LS Raynor

23RD DEC 09

Chelsea

———————————

A
Short History
of Europe

www.pocketessentials.com

A
Short History
of Europe

From Charlemagne to the Treaty of Lisbon

GORDON KERR

POCKET ESSENTIALS

First published in 2009 by Pocket Essentials
PO Box 394, Harpenden, Herts, AL5 1XJ
www.pocketessentials.com

A CIP catalogue record for this book is available from the British Library.

ISBN 978-1-84243-330-0

2 4 6 8 10 9 7 5 3 1

Typeset by Avocet Typeset, Chilton, Aylesbury, Bucks
Printed and bound in Great Britain by JH Haynes Ltd, Yeovil, Somerset

In memory of
William Kerr
Helen Kerr
and Dennis Baker

'I grew up in Europe, where the history comes from'
— Eddie Izzard

Contents

Introduction

What is Europe?

Firstly, of course, it is a continent. A continent made up of countless disparate peoples, races and countries. A continent of different ideas, philosophies, religions and attitudes and just as each individual country is many things and not one, so, too, is the continent of Europe.

Nonetheless, it has a common thread of history that runs through it, stitching the lands of its past and present together into one fabric. Great institutions such as the Church of Rome, the Holy Roman Empire, the individual monarchies, trade organisations and social movements that have existed during its history have welded it together and sometimes prevented anarchy from destroying the achievements of the many great men and women that Europe has produced. At other times, of course, these very institutions have been at the heart of the war and strife that have threatened to reduce the continent of Europe to ruin. The wars of the twentieth century, for instance, founded on imperial aspiration and national and racial prejudice, left a continent ravaged by death, its inhabitants horrified by man's potential for evil.

Perhaps Europe is also an attitude, a quest for improvement and achievement. From the countries of the continent, ships sailed on great voyages of discovery, opening up the world for exploration and settlement. Alongside the terrible exploitation that often accompanied the ensuing imperialism, much that was good was also achieved and the world became a bigger place. In the fields of science and the arts, Europe and Europeans have been at the heart of innovation, creativity and discovery. Great Europeans such as Copernicus, Newton, Leonardo and Shakespeare have illuminated the world's learning and enhanced the lives of everyone on the planet.

If Europe is the sum of its disparate parts, it is also the culmination of millennia of history. But it was as it emerged from the Dark Ages that it began to become the entity we know now. Charlemagne took the first steps on the road and, within a few decades of his death, the great powers of the continent began to form when the Treaty of Verdun was signed in 843. By this treaty, the three sons of Louis the Pious, who had succeeded Charlemagne in 814, divided the Carolingian Empire between them. For the first time, the kingdom of France became a distinct state (known as West Francia) with Charles the Bald as monarch; Lothair became king of Middle Francia, comprising the Low Countries, Lorraine, Alsace, Burgundy, Provence and the kingdom of Italy; East Francia, now Germany and other regions to the east, was to be ruled by Louis the German.

Perhaps above all, however, Europe is an idea. From almost the beginning of its recorded history, men have harboured aspirations to make this vast territory one. The Romans came close and, eight centuries later, Charlemagne laid the foundations for a great European state when he brought into being the Holy Roman Empire – an empire different to any other in that, through the Church in Rome, it enjoyed the approval of God. In later attempts, Napoleon overreached himself, as did Adolf Hitler.

Today Europe is as close as it ever has been to the dream of unity. The European Union, begun as a common market of six countries in 1957 with the signing of the Treaty of Rome, is an ever-expanding club which every state in Europe wants to join. The new nations of the east, risen from the ashes of communism and eager to share in the wealth of the continent, are especially anxious to become members.

As Europe moves painfully ever closer to a greater degree of union, it is a good time to examine the events, people and thinking that have brought it to this point.

The End of Darkness

Charlemagne: Father of Europe

On Christmas Day 800, as Charlemagne (747–814), King of the Franks, knelt in prayer in St Peter's Basilica in Rome, Pope Leo III (Pope 795–816) placed a crown on his head, hailing him as *Imperator Romanorum* ('Emperor of the Romans'). Charlemagne would later claim that the coronation was unexpected, although he was almost certainly being disingenuous in doing so. Unexpected or not, this coronation marked a defining moment in the history of Europe.

In one sense, Leo was simply rewarding the 53-year-old Frankish monarch for coming to his aid. A few years previously, the Pope, unpopular with the Roman nobility, had been set upon by rivals during a papal procession and had come close to having his eyes and tongue cut out. Following his narrow escape, he turned to Charlemagne for help. Charlemagne had obliged, travelling to Rome and restoring Leo to the papal throne.

It is likely, however, that Leo had other things on his mind when he placed the bejewelled crown on the king's blond locks. For a start, he was ensuring that he and his successors would enjoy the continued protection of the Franks. However, he was also filling the imperial vacancy created by events in Byzantium from where, since the fall of the Roman Empire, the Roman Emperor had traditionally come. The ongoing 'Iconoclasm Crisis' and the instability of Empress Irene (ruled as Empress

Consort, regent and Empress 775–802) had led Leo to sever his links with the Byzantines and to consider the position of emperor vacant.

Thus, the Franks were now established as the great power of Europe, but how had they achieved this position of supremacy?

The rise of Frankish power can be traced back to 751 when the Lombards, in pursuit of their ambitions to rule the whole of Italy, conquered Ravenna, the Italian seat of the Byzantine Exarch, or governor. The Pope at the time, Stephen II (Pope from 752 to 757), asked the Franks, then the only Catholic people outside Italy, for help. Pepin the Short (ruled 751–68), Charlemagne's father, obliged the papacy, just as his son later would, and drove the Lombards from Ravenna. Pepin already held high office in Frankish circles – Mayor of the Palace or *majordomo* and Duke of the Franks – but his reward from a grateful Pope would elevate him still further. Stephen announced his recognition of Pepin as King of the Franks, at the expense of the weak Childeric III (ruled 743–51), the last king of the previous ruling dynasty, the Merovingians. The Carolingian dynasty – named after its greatest member, Charlemagne – had begun and the King of the Franks would henceforth be chosen by God, in the shape of his representative on earth, the Pope.

On Pepin's death in 768, his kingdom was split between his two sons, Charlemagne and Carloman (ruled 751–71) as was customary under the rule of partible inheritance employed by the Franks. When Carloman died in 771 – of a severe nosebleed, according to some sources – Charlemagne was left as sole monarch and he began the creation of the greatest Frankish state of the Middle Ages, uniting the two halves of the kingdom of his forebears. These were Neustria (generally speaking, most of modern-day France) and Austrasia (eastern France, western

Germany, Belgium, Luxembourg and the Netherlands). Charlemagne was not satisfied with these territories, however, and, during his reign, he fought some 53 campaigns in order to extend his vast realm. South of the Alps, he conquered the kingdom of the Lombards; he added Saxony in 774; Bavaria in 788; Carinthia in 799; the March of Brittany in 786 and, in 797, the Marca Hispanica, a buffer zone at the edge of his southern province of Septimania, designed to keep the Umayyad Moors of the Iberian Peninsula at bay.

He travelled incessantly and his government was itinerant. Nonetheless, he established an effective system of governance for all the disparate nations of his empire. The top echelon was occupied by a network of some 300 *comitates* or Counties, each of which was headed by an imperial lieutenant or Count. These officials were often supervised by local bishops and royal legates, known as *Missi Dominici*, who toured the realm to ensure that the royal will was being followed. Charlemagne was careful, at the same time, to ensure that local customs were respected and, in reality, local leaders retained much of their power. The important people of the realm – officials, bishops and the rich – swore oaths of loyalty at annual assemblies which took place at Aachen. A new elite, international class emerged, basking in royal favour and often united in marriage.

Charlemagne also encouraged a cultural revival, employing the greatest scholars of the day to facilitate it. The English monk, scholar, poet and teacher, Alcuin of York (735–804), was invited to the court and became its most prominent teacher. Many of the most notable minds of the Carolingian era were taught there by him. Even Charlemagne took courses at his celebrated Palace Academy. Others such as the grammarian Peter of Pisa (744–99) and the theologian Agobard of Lyons (769–840) also contributed to the intellectual renaissance fostered by the

Emperor, revising the text of the Bible and publishing grammars, histories and ballads. In architecture, too, there was innovation and change. Carolingian architecture threw off the pervasive Byzantine influence, initiating the style that, with its round arches and groin vaults, would later become known as Romanesque.

Charlemagne revived the ancient term 'Europe' to distinguish his lands from those of Byzantium and of the pagans beyond his borders. However, it was not destined to last and, when he finally died on 28 January 814, the concept died with him. So too did his empire. As was customary, his son, Louis the Pious (ruled 813–40), had been crowned co-emperor in 813 to avoid a destructive succession dispute on Charlemagne's death. However, when Louis died in 840, the kingdom was shared between the late king's sons. The Treaty of Verdun in 843 allowed for this division.

The western lands of the empire, known as West Francia, were given to Charles the Bald (ruled 840–77); Lothair (ruled 840–55) became king of Middle Francia, comprising the Low Countries, Lorraine, Alsace, Burgundy, Provence and the kingdom of Italy; East Francia, now Germany and other regions to the east, was to be ruled by the appropriately named Louis the German (843–76).

The great nations of Europe began to take shape.

Invaders: Vikings, Magyars and Ottoman Turks

The empire left by Charlemagne had become fragmented and soon descended into petty fiefdoms and internecine warfare. By the last years of the ninth century, a new kingdom had emerged in upper Burgundy and Count Boso was effectively king of lower Burgundy. Italy had been ravaged for many years by invasion by

Byzantines, Neustrians and Austrasians and any political authority that had once existed had long since been eroded. It was against such a background that a new terror arrived, a terror that would destroy people's faith in central authority still further. The Frankish kings, who were supposed to provide protection, seemed incapable of doing so against the new pagan threat from the north – the Vikings.

No one is entirely sure why the Norsemen set out on their initial voyages of conquest. It may have been due to over-crowding in their homeland but some suggest that they were merely an adventurous race in search of new opportunities. Whatever the reason, they raided and settled in Europe for some 200 years, creating new states and often establishing themselves through time amongst the ruling elite of the countries they invaded. Above all, they created prosperity for their native lands, establishing political power for northern Europe for the first time.

The Swedes, known as Varangians, headed east, plundering the lands of the Baltic, the Bay of Riga and the Gulf of Finland and establishing camps at Wolin on the Oder, on the Vistula and at Novgorod in modern-day northwest Russia. They even made it as far as Constantinople. The Danes and the Norwegians turned their attention to the south and west, causing panic in Ireland, Great Britain, Germany, Holland, France and as far as the Mediterranean and Greece.

The *Anglo-Saxon Chronicle* – the late ninth-century manuscript that narrates the history of the Anglo-Saxons – gives 789 as the date of the first Viking raid on Britain. That summer, three Norwegian ships entered Portland Bay in Dorset. Four years later, Viking raiders attacked and plundered the monastery on the island of Lindisfarne, off the northeast coast of England, appropriating church treasures, killing many monks and carrying off as slaves those they did not kill. Two years later it was the turn of the holy Scottish isle of Iona. The Vikings would return again and again to these places. In 875 the monks of Lindisfarne finally decamped, taking the relics of Saint Cuthbert with them. They would remain an itinerant community for several decades.

The Danes were the principal invaders. In 841, they took advantage of the political uncertainty caused by the death of Louis the Pious, as the empire occupied itself with the fallout from the division of the empire between his three sons. Employing their customary strategy, they sailed up the river Seine to the city of Rouen which was ruthlessly attacked and plundered. Bordeaux was captured in 847, remaining hostage to the Vikings for many years. As became the custom, the West Frankish king, Charles the Bald, paid them off. Unfortunately for him, and the terrified people of his kingdom, the raids continued. Charles ordered every settlement to prepare itself with defences, fortifications and troops but it was to no avail and, when 40,000 Vikings laid siege to Paris itself, Charles was forced to pay them off with 700lbs of gold. The Vikings retired to Burgundy.

Paying them off seemed to be the only way to stop them, especially in Britain where the Viking invasions had a huge impact on everyday life as well as on the political life of the country. In 828, the house of Wessex had become pre-eminent when King Egbert (ruled 802–39) was recognised as *Bretwalda* – overlord of Britain. It was not long, however, before the Danes began to challenge Wessex superiority and Alfred the Great (ruled 871–99) spent his entire reign as King of Wessex fending off the Scandinavian threat. Eventually, after defeating the Danish warlord, Guthrum (died c. 890) at the Battle of Edington, Alfred signed a treaty with the Danes that established the borders of their respective territories. The land under

Danish control and subject to Danish law – an area roughly to the north of a line drawn between London and Chester – became known as the *Danelaw*. Eric Bloodaxe (895–954), the last Danish king of the Northern Viking kingdom, was driven out of Northumbria in 954, but ultimate power in England would continue to be disputed by the Danes and the House of Wessex until 1066.

Events in France would prove fatal for the struggle for supremacy in England. In 911, the French king, Charles the Simple (ruled 893–922), signed a treaty with the Viking leader, Rollo (c. 860–932). When Rollo had invaded Normandy, Charles realised that there was little point in continuing the struggle. If he paid the Vikings off, they would only return. Consequently, he gave Rollo and his followers the lands in Normandy that they had conquered on condition they fight off any raids by their Viking brothers. Rollo became ruler and possibly Duke of Normandy. One hundred and fifty-five years later, his great-great-great grandson, William the Conqueror (ruled 1066–87) would become King of England after defeating King Harold II (ruled 1066) at the Battle of Hastings. The Normans would also extend their reach as far as southern Italy, conquered in the 1050s by Robert Guiscard (c. 1015–85) who was descended from the norsemen who had sailed up the Seine several hundred years earlier.

It was not only the threat from the north that made Europe an unsettling place to live at the end of the Dark Ages. From the east came the Magyars, the last of the nomadic tribes to invade central Europe. Overwhelmed by their neighbours, the Pechenegs, and their ally, the Tsar of the Bulgars, they migrated over the Carpathian Mountains to the west, settling finally in the Hungarian plains. As rapacious as the Vikings, they cut a swathe through the Carolingian Empire from 895 until 955, extracting huge ransoms and tribute monies. Later invasions brought the greatest nomadic empire of them all to Europe – the Mongols, also known as Tatars. In the thirteenth century, Genghis Khan (1162–1227) ruled a vast empire stretching from the Pacific to the Black Sea, the largest empire in history; from 1336 to 1405, the Mongol Emperor Tamerlane ruled from Delhi in India to the Aegean. Meanwhile, the Ottoman Turks had arrived in the eleventh century and would wield influence in Eastern Europe for the next 800 years.

Such instability only served to weaken central power and destroy confidence in the Frankish monarchies and the end result was feudalism. However, just as Charlemagne's great empire was created partly to protect against invasion, the incursions of the Vikings, the Magyars and all the others led to the creation of the Holy Roman Empire and the Tsardom of Moscow.

The Byzantine Empire

As the Frankish empire began to wane, so did another former great power begin an astonishing resurgence. It had been the Emperor Theodosius (ruled 379–95) – the last emperor to rule the Roman Empire in its entirety – who had made the fateful decision to split the empire in two on his death in 395, dividing it between his two sons, Honorius (ruled 395–423) in the West and Arcadius (ruled 395–408) in the East. As various invaders overran the Western half in the course of the next century, the Eastern Empire was left relatively unscathed.

In the sixth century, the Eastern Emperor, Justinian I (ruled 527–65), had overseen an expansion of his territories but, during the next two centuries, his descendants had lost much of these gains. In the eighth and ninth centuries, the empire had been riven by a debilitating iconoclasm dispute – the issue being whether or not it was right to worship icons. It was destabilising and sometimes violent and the empire reached its lowest ebb.

Towards the end of the ninth century, however, the Macedonian dynasty seized the throne. Basil I (ruled 867–86), a former peasant horse-breaker, who had risen to a position of prominence at the imperial court, came to power by murdering the previous emperor, Michael III (ruled 842–67), in September 867. Despite such an inglorious beginning to his reign, Basil launched a remarkable rebirth of Byzantine fortunes, a rebirth perpetuated by his successors, Leo VI the Wise (ruled 886–912), Constantine VII Porphyrogenitus (ruled 913–59), Romanos II (ruled 959–63), Nicephoros II Phocas (ruled 963–69), John I Tzimisces (ruled 969–76) and Basil II (ruled 976–1025), known as the 'Bulgar Slayer'.

In the tenth century the Byzantines strove once again to expand their territory. The Arabs had traumatised the empire by taking Thessalonika in 904 and massacring its inhabitants. Sicily and Crete had also fallen to them at the start of the tenth century. From 961, however, Byzantium began to fight back. Under the generalship of the future emperor, Nicephoros, Crete was retaken and the Mediterranean was freed from the scourge of Arab pirates. Nicephoros conquered Cilicia – the Anatolian Peninsula – and advanced as far as Syria where he captured Aleppo. During this campaign, he earned the nickname, 'The Pale Death of the Saracens'. Even better, from his conquests he also earned a fortune for himself and for the empire.

Others continued these heroic deeds and, by the beginning of the eleventh century, a Byzantine army stood at the gates of Jerusalem. The empire also extended its authority into Armenia and into Caucasian Georgia to the north. It had not been easy as there were threats from all sides. Slavs and people called Avars, a powerful, multi-ethnic, Turkic tribal confederation, arrived from northern Russia, the Arabs were mustering on the eastern border and Lombards attacked Byzantine territories in Italy. Their greatest rivals, however, were their neighbours, the Bulgars. Their mutual religion, Christianity, had helped to maintain a shaky peace between the two but, when Simeon I (ruled 893–927) came to the Bulgarian throne, that peace was shattered and a period of hostilities began. Simeon created a vast empire, stretching between the Adriatic, the Aegean and the Black Sea, to rival that of the Byzantines and he styled himself Tsar. The wars he began continued until the Byzantines comprehensively defeated the Bulgars at the Battle of Kleidion in 1014. Basil's revenge on the defeated army was, indeed, terrible. He is said to have taken 15,000 of them prisoner and divided them into groups of 100. He then blinded every man in each of the groups, except for one soldier whom he left with one good eye so that he could lead his 99 blind colleagues back to Bulgaria. As he watched his sorry army arrive home, Tsar Samuil (ruled 997–1014) is reported to have been so shocked that he suffered a heart attack and died.

The Bulgar threat was no more. In 1018, they surrendered unconditionally and were incorporated into the Byzantine Empire that now included the whole of the Balkans and had the Danube as its northern frontier. The Bulgars would remain under Byzantine control for 150 years. Territorial expansion, economic stability and the security of its borders now allowed the Byzantine Empire to develop militarily, politically, socially and culturally. The empire was organised into military zones known as 'themes' and it was constantly prepared to go to war. Cleverly, however, the Byzantines also sent missionaries out to their enemies, believing that a shared religion would reduce the chance of war. Moreover, the imperial court presided over a bureaucracy that ensured uniform systems and legislation were enjoyed in every part of the Empire.

Constantinople became the cultural centre of the medieval universe with an intellectual elite, led by Photios (810–93), professor and patriarch of the city, teaching and working there. Many great works were produced and Byzantine scholars also performed the valuable function of preserving numerous important works of Greek and Roman antiquity. Architecture, painting, mosaics and craftsmanship also underwent a renaissance. Architecture began to show a concern for external appearance and strove for an aesthetic perfection; painting became symbolic and abstract. Byzantine cultural influence spread across the continent.

Eventually, however, the empire went into decline. Clergy and landowners enjoyed great privilege and taxation weighed very heavily on the less well-off. The economy began to suffer and the empire became less able to fend off external threats from the Seljuk Turks, who had settled in Asia Minor, and the Normans who, under Robert Guiscard, had seized parts of southern Italy in 1071. Increasingly decadent emperors became more interested in palace intrigue than in governing the empire and, as soldier-farmers began to pay not to be in the army, mercenaries had to be hired to fight the Byzantine Empire's wars.

In 1057, army commander Isaac Komnenos (ruled 1057–59) forced Emperor Michael VI (ruled 1056–57) to abdicate and seized power. The empire would flower again briefly in the twelfth century but, in 1204, the city of Constantinople was sacked after the emperor had failed to pay money to the forces of the Fourth Crusade and the lands of the empire were split up. The golden age was long gone.

Western Europe: The Tenth and Eleventh Centuries

In their rampage through Europe in the first half of the tenth century, the Magyar invaders overwhelmed Italy, Bavaria, Saxony and Moravia. They represented such an ongoing and expensive threat – through the ransoms and tribute payments they demanded – that the German nobles abandoned their customary in-fighting and united against them. In 955, during yet another invasion of Bavaria, Otto I (Holy Roman Emperor 962–73), King of the Germans, defeated them at Lechfeld, near Augsburg. It was such a decisive victory that it brought the Magyar threat to an end. The nomadic Magyars returned to the plains of modern-day Hungary where they settled and were eventually converted to Christianity by Byzantine missionaries.

They had contributed, however, to the future shape of Europe. Their conquest of Greater Moravia helped to create a number of independent states that exist to this day – Hungary, Bohemia, Poland, Croatia, Serbia and Austria. They also played a major role in the creation of the prevailing power of the next few centuries – the Holy Roman Empire. The German princes had united behind Otto and, after the Battle of Lechfeld, he was raised high on their shields as they proclaimed him Emperor.

Otto had become King of Germany in 936. He was the son of Henry the Fowler (ruled 919–36) who had turned Saxony into a force to be reckoned with by creating the eastern Marches, installing settlements and building walled towns in order to prevent invasion from the Danes, Slavs and Magyars. Critically, however, he managed to establish a link with Italy through the Pope. John XII (Pope 955–64) was losing a war against Berengar II (ruled 950–63), King of Italy, and he turned to Otto for help. In return, the Pope promised he would crown the Saxon as Holy Roman Emperor in a formal ceremony in

Rome. Otto jumped at the opportunity to obtain God's approval for his title but he added one very important condition. He insisted on having control over all church appointments. John reluctantly agreed and, on 2 February 962, Otto was crowned Holy Roman Emperor. The restored Empire would endure for more than 800 years, until it was finally dismantled by Napoleon in 1806.

Before long, however, the Pope began to regret his decision and became increasingly resentful of Otto's power. He sent emissaries to both the Magyars and the Byzantines, urging them to form a league against the Saxons. A disgruntled Otto returned to Rome and deposed John, installing Leo VIII (Pope 963–65). Leo, not even a clergyman, was ordained into the priesthood one day and elected Pope the next. As soon as Otto left, however, civil war broke out in Rome and John was restored to the papal throne. When he died shortly after and was replaced by Benedict V (Pope 964–66), Otto returned to Rome once more to depose this latest incumbent. This time, he made the Romans promise never to elect a pontiff without the approval of the Emperor.

Otto's imperial title did not impress the Byzantines and they were even more disturbed by the fact that, by 972, Otto had conquered all of their territories in Italy. Cleverly, however, he offered to hand them back in return for a mutual recognition of titles. He cemented the relationship by marrying his son to Theophanu, niece of a previous Byzantine Emperor, John I Tzimisces (ruled c. 925–76). Thus the concept of one, unified Roman Empire disappeared forever.

Otto II (ruled 967–83), son of Otto the Great, did continue to harbour dreams of ruling over a larger realm but few shared them. Henry II (ruled 1014–24), the last of the Saxon dynasty, was too preoccupied with other matters to entertain thoughts of a single empire. He had to deal with civil wars in Germany, skirmishes with the Slavs on their common border and, on the other side of the empire, occasional wars with the French.

The French had their own problems, but their succession issues were settled in 987 when the last Carolingian monarch died without issue. Hugh Capet (ruled 987–96), son of Hugh le Grand, Duke of France (898–956), a powerful landowner in the Île-de-France, was elected by the kingdom's feudal vassals who saw him as weak and easily manipulated. Initially, the new king's power was limited only to the royal domain around Paris, a small area of approximately 400 square miles, stretching from Senlis in the north to Orléans to the south. It has to be remembered just how fragmented France, or West Francia, was at this time. There were as many as 150 different currencies in circulation and a dozen different languages were spoken. Consequently, Hugh Capet's reign was punctuated by power struggles with his feudal lords. He did, however, succeed in having his son, Robert, crowned early in his reign – on the pretext that he might be killed during one of his campaigns. Thus he ensured the survival of the Capetians, a survival that was further helped by three centuries of male heirs which prevented any succession issues. The dynasty was to last 800 years, its uninterrupted rule being brought to an end by the French Revolution, but even then it returned after Napoleon's demise and reigned for a further 33 years, from 1815 until 1848.

England, meanwhile, enjoyed the reign of one of its greatest kings. Alfred, the fourth son of King Æthelwulf to become king, ruled the southern Anglo-Saxon kingdom of Wessex from 871 until his death in 899, defeating the Danes and bringing much-needed stability and order to his kingdom. Athelstan (ruled 924–39) not only established a single administrative and legislative system but, having won the submission of King Constantine II of the Scots (ruled 900–43), felt able to style himself 'King of

All Britain'. The Vikings were never very far away, however, and the payment of tributes – *Danegeld* – was crippling to the royal purse. Finally, the Danish Canute the Great (ruled 1016–35), son of Sweyn Forkbeard who had briefly held the throne of England, subjugated the country with a raid in 1014. Canute now ruled a vast northern empire from the Baltic to Greenland. He reigned in England until his death in 1035 but, by 1042, rivalry amongst his successors led to the election by the Witan – England's governing council – of an Anglo-Saxon king again. This was Edward the Confessor (ruled 1043–66), the last king of England from the House of Wessex. Although he did divide the country into counties, his reign was marked by the increasing power of the nobles and his death without an heir led to the strife depicted in the Bayeux Tapestry. In 1066, Duke William of Normandy defeated and killed King Harold II at the Battle of Hastings and took the throne as King William the Conqueror.

Religion

From the ninth to the twelfth centuries, countries fell to Christianity like dominoes. Moravia, Bohemia, Bulgaria, Hungary, Poland and even Kievan Rus', colonised by Varangians (pagan Scandinavians), were all converted and some were rewarded with crowns from the Pope. Even heathen Scandinavia, whose warlike ways seemed to be very much at odds with the tenets of the Christian church, began to succumb during the eleventh century. Given, however, that missionary work was central to both the Greek and Latin churches, it was fairly inevitable that their teaching would make inroads into the various cultures with which the missionaries came into contact.

First to convert was Moravia, situated in the east of the

present-day Czech Republic. In 862, two Greek brothers, Cyril (827–69) and Methodius (826–82), both later canonised, were sent by the Patriarch of Constantinople to carry out missionary work in opposition to German priests already there. King Rastislav (ruled 846–70) had obtained his throne with the help of the Frankish monarch Louis the German but he was eager to assert his independence from the Frankish Empire. St Cyril devised the Glagolitic alphabet, the first alphabet to be used for Slavonic manuscripts. Its descendant alphabet – the Cyrillic – is still in use in many countries today. Cyril also translated the Bible.

In Bulgaria, Boris I (ruled 852–89) toyed with both churches before agreeing to be baptised by the Patriarch of Constantinople, while in Bohemia successive kings alternated in their religious allegiances. Eventually, after more than a century under the Premyslid dynasty, when both the Slavonic and Latin liturgy were performed, the Latin won out. Since Bohemia was a fief of the Empire and affiliated to the German church, this was always the likeliest outcome.

The mission of Cyril and Methodius provided Poland with its first Christian connection and the chief of the Vistulanian tribe – the people who lived along the banks of Poland's longest river, the Vistula – was baptised in 875. His people's association with the Slavonic rite continued until the twelfth century. In the north, however, it took until the tenth century to convert people from their pagan practices and it was the Latin Church that succeeded in doing so. In 965, Mieszko I (ruled c.962–92), in the face of a surge of Saxon power following their decisive defeat of the Magyars at the Battle of Lechfeld, formed an alliance with the Czechs. Mieszko married a Czech princess and was baptised. By 1000, Wielkopolska (Great Poland) had been joined to Malopolska (Little Poland) in the south and Mieszko's successor,

Boleslaw the Brave (ruled 992–1025), was given the first crown of Poland by Pope Benedict VIII (Pope 1012–1024). Poland would repay this gift by becoming and remaining the shining light of Catholicism in Eastern Europe.

When the Magyars were defeated at the Battle of Lechfeld, Hungary came under German control and the Latin Church held sway. The bond with the Empire was confirmed by the baptism of Magyar Prince Géza (ruled 972–97) in 975 and the subsequent marriage of his son István (ruled 997–1038) to a Bavarian princess.

For the Varangians of Kievan Rus', conversion to Christianity was merely the pragmatic thing to do. Vladimir, Prince of Kiev (ruled 980–1018), was certainly no Christian. He had murdered his brother and had taken numerous wives. He had considered all the major religions but settled on Christianity as the necessary price for persuading the Eastern Empire to hire the 6,000 soldiers of his Varangian Guard as mercenaries. Missionaries spread from Kiev to Minsk, Novgorod and Polotsk.

Scandinavia did not welcome Christianity with open arms. In Denmark, Sweyn Forkbeard (ruled 986–1014), whose father Harold Bluetooth (ruled 940–86) had been baptised and then excommunicated, was the driving force. Then Canute the Great sent Anglo-Saxon missionaries to try to convert Scandinavia. In Norway, Olaf Haroldson (ruled 1016–28) converted his country by nefarious means, coercing and paying off reluctant nobles on his way to national sainthood. Meanwhile, in Sweden, following the baptism in 1008 of King Olaf Skötkonung (ruled 995–1022), civil war broke out between pagans and Christians and lasted for a hundred years.

The two Churches, Latin and Greek, managed to coexist for centuries, never fully cooperating and enduring endless disputes and crises – such as the long-running Iconoclasm

Crisis. In 1043, however, a critical moment for Christianity arrived. Patriarch Michael Kerularios (1000–59) was engaged in a dispute with Pope Leo IX (Pope 1049–54) over a number of issues, but primarily the use of unleavened bread in the Eucharist. He had already riled the Pope by closing all the Latin churches in Constantinople after falling out with the Byzantine governor of southern Italy. Leo sent the papal legate Humbert of Silva Candida (1015–61) to Constantinople to press his claims of supremacy over the Eastern Church but the Patriarch spurned the legate and was summarily excommunicated, the excommunication document being laid by Humbert on the altar of Hagia Sophia. The Patriarch retaliated and, Leo having died in the meantime, excommunicated the legates. The two churches had reached an impasse. The schism between East and West has never been repaired. Since 1054, Europe has been split between the Catholic lands in the West and the Orthodox lands to the East.

Feudalism

Since the fall of the Roman Empire, the way that people interacted with each other had changed. In Roman times the relationship that mattered was that of the individual to the state, the Empire. In the absence of that impersonal central authority, what began to matter was people's relationship to each other within a system known to us as 'feudal', although the term was unknown to those that lived at the time. The dictionary definition of feudalism is:

> a system of social organisation prevalent in Western Europe in the Middle Ages in which powerful land-owning lords granted degrees of privilege and protection to lesser subjects

holding a range of positions within a rigid social hierarchy. (Chambers Dictionary 10th Edition, published Chambers Harrap Publishers, 2006.)

Although this definition of the word is not absolute – in practice, it varied from one region or country to another – feudalism was basically a hierarchical system by which one man became the 'vassal' of another, more powerful person. The king was a vassal of the emperor, the aristocrats were lords to their vassals, the knights; agricultural workers, 'villeins', were vassals of the knights, and below them, at the bottom of the heap, were the peasants, or serfs. Thus, in this system, each man knew his position, a position that remained the same for his entire life. Above all, he knew what his relationship was to the others in the complex social network of the Middle Ages.

Each person, from the most powerful to the very poorest and weakest, had something to contribute. There were two currencies – land and military service. The lord loaned his vassal land – a 'fief' – to work and to live off and the vassal provided his master with loyalty and service, often in battle.

The vassalage ceremony was codified in France at the end of the eighth century. People saw that feudalism was a way of ensuring security in turbulent times and provided the means to raise local militia to deal with incursions and lawlessness. The feudal system was an absolute necessity if a sizeable warrior class of knights was to be maintained. Equipment and the upkeep of retinues and castles were all very expensive and feudalism provided a framework within which they could be supported. The first indications of the system emerged in northwestern Gaul, or France, but it spread quickly to the Rhine and across the rest of Europe. The ninth century saw Charlemagne's knights bringing it to northern and central Italy and it was William the

Conqueror who introduced it to England after 1066, a little later than the rest of Christendom.

The reason for its development was rooted in, amongst other things, a shift in the power base in Europe. The emergence of lordships and the building of castles and fortified towns from the tenth century onwards reflected people's growing distrust of the previously all-powerful central authority wielded by the kings and counts, as well as their fear that they were powerless to prevent incursions by the various invaders – Vikings, Magyars and Saracens – who were plaguing Europe. Castles sprang up on vantage points in strategic positions and, together with fortified towns and villages, became centres of power – limited, in geographic scope, but manageable – to which people gravitated for security and to earn their keep.

Although it was not until the eleventh century that castles became the stone-walled, fortified keeps with turrets with which we are so familiar, they provided the hub for local people. The lords owned the land and wielded complete authority over those who had sworn loyalty to them as well as over other free men. They had the right to gather taxes and wield judiciary power. They were in receipt of services from their vassals – effectively forced labour in the form of upkeep of the castle itself or work on the land. The vassals would also have to use the lord's mill and his ovens, and at his price.

Although feudalism arrived at different times across Europe the 50 years from 980 to 1030 can be looked upon as a period of feudal revolution. The role of the knight changed during this time. Until then, he was a violent provider of trouble and disorder. The Church changed this image, however, bringing an end to the relentless violence of the warlords. The knighthood was formalised, becoming a kind of club to which admittance could only be gained following a ceremony or ritual conducted by religious officials. The knight's weapons were blessed and he swore to defend the Church, the weak and the poor. Thus, by the end of the twelfth century, the knight had become an ideal figure, both ethically and religiously, and the concept of chivalry, with its connotations of courtly love, honour and virtue had emerged as something to which to aspire.

Feeding a Growing Population

The emergence of feudalism coincided with the beginning of a period of population growth. There were around 38 million people in Europe in the tenth century, rising to more than 75 million by the fourteenth. Better farming meant that more people could be supported. Therefore, there were more people to work. Apart from the sheer number of workers, productivity was increased by a number of factors. Firstly, improved techniques in iron-working allowed better tools to be crafted and made available accessories such as parts for ploughs, horseshoes and nails. The invention of the heavy plough, pulled by horse, permitted the preparation of low-lying, more fertile land that had previously been impossible to plough. The introduction of three-year crop rotation had a dramatic impact, reducing fallow land from 50 per cent of a holding to 30 per cent. It also became possible to cultivate spring crops such as oats. The availability of oats, in turn, allowed more efficient horse-breeding.

Carolingian Europe had been, in the main, heavily forested with groups of people living in communities separated by vast swathes of unpopulated and undeveloped land. People lived off the resources of the forest, hunting, gathering or breeding pigs. Now, with so many people on hand, deforestation was possible. The open-field system became popular throughout the northern and central areas of the continent – each manor or village owned a number of large fields that were farmed in strips by individual families.

The farming improvements led to a social and cultural revolution. People's eating habits changed, as grain supplanted the food obtained from the forest. Land was reclaimed from forests and marshes to be cultivated and people began to move, extending the frontiers of Christendom. Large numbers of peasants emigrated from Germany and the Low Countries to the sparsely populated lands beyond the Elbe to the east where there was freedom, villages were autonomous and, more importantly, rents were low.

Church Reform and the Investiture Dispute

The Church had become increasingly secular during the Carolingian period. The Emperor's authority was derived directly from God and no one questioned his right to approve the appointment of bishops. Bishops wielded secular power, were involved in government and were landowners through the benefices they received. Around 1030, there was agitation for reform within the Church, especially from the monasteries who saw priests and bishops becoming too involved in the temporal world and devoting insufficient time to the spiritual. Many priests did not adhere to the rule of celibacy, openly living with women, and many were guilty of simony – the ecclesiastical crime of paying for holy offices or positions in the hierarchy of a church.

The great reformer, Gregory VII, became Pope in 1073 and immediately began to make waves. In 1075, he published the *Dictatus Papae*, a series of 27 axiomatic statements embodying the reform that he espoused. Critically, he stated that the pontiff had supreme legislative and judicial power within Christendom and, 'That it may be permitted to him to depose emperors'. Within a short time, he went a step further, excommunicating all secular rulers who made church appointments without reference to the ecclesiastical authority. It did not take a genius to see that a major conflict was about to erupt between Pope and Emperor over one simple question. Who was in charge?

Battle was soon joined. Emperor Henry IV, King of Germany from 1056 and Holy Roman Emperor from 1084 until he was forced to abdicate in 1105, excommunicated the Pope and appointed an Antipope, Clement III. Gregory responded by excommunicating Henry and rebellious German princes elected a new Emperor, Rupert of Swabia. So, the Empire was now in the unhappy situation of having not only two Popes but also two Emperors. Henry, having been abandoned by his supporters, decided that humility was the best way out of the crisis and, with great drama, turned up at the Pope's court in Canossa, clad in the rags of a penitent and begging forgiveness. Of course, as soon as he had been forgiven and had returned to Germany, he renewed his plotting against the Pope.

The dispute rumbled on long after Henry IV and Gregory VII had left the stage, eventually being brought to a fairly unsatisfactory conclusion with the Concordat of Worms in 1122. Pope Calixtus II (Pope 1119–24) and Emperor Henry V (ruled 1111–25) agreed that the elections of bishops and abbots in Germany were to be held in the Emperor's presence so that he could mediate in the case of dispute. He was, however, disallowed from claiming payment for this service and was not permitted to invest them with the ring and crozier, the two symbols of their spiritual power. The secular authority had been removed from the process of selecting Church officials.

The dispute would not go away entirely but there is little doubt that it represented a key moment in the development of Europe. According to one authority:

'The investiture controversy had shattered the early-medieval equilibrium and ended the interpenetration of *ecclesia* and *mundus*. Medieval kingship, which had been largely the creation of ecclesiastical ideals and personnel, was forced to develop new institutions and sanctions. The result during the late eleventh and early twelfth centuries was the first instance of a secular bureaucratic state whose essential components appeared in the Anglo-Norman monarchy.' (Norman Cantor – *The Civilization of the Middle Ages*, 'The Entrenchment of Secular Leadership', p 395.)

While the reform movement had had the wind taken out of its sails, however, the increasingly hierarchical nature of the Church soon disillusioned many who began to make their own reforms. One of the results of this was an increase in what the Church called heresies.

Crusades, Plagues and Heresies

The Crusades

By its very nature, the era of feudalism, with its fortified castles and villages, warrior knights and power-hungry lords, was a violent and bloody time. The Church had introduced the Peace and Truce of God, using spiritual sanctions to limit the violence that was endemic in Europe. This first real effort at civilising European society using non-violent means was initially proclaimed in 989 and persisted in one form or another until the thirteenth century.

Pope Urban II (Pope 1088–99) conceived of another way to stop Christian killing Christian. He decided to direct the violence of European society on to another target – the Saracens. In November 1095, he crossed the Alps to give what has been described as one of the most important speeches in European history, at the Council of Clermont, a synod of churchmen and laymen. He had called the synod to discuss a plea he had received from the Byzantine Emperor, Alexius I Komnenos (ruled 1081–1118), for military assistance against the new threat of the Seljuk Turks who were attacking Byzantium from the east.

The Turks had initially plundered the Arab world, taking first Baghdad and then, in 1071, Jerusalem. The Turkish leader, Sultan Alp Arslan (ruled 1059–72), by then head of an empire stretching from the Oxus to the Tigris, was en route to Syria, when he decided to attack Byzantium. The Byzantine Emperor of the time, Romanos IV Diogenes, personally led out an army against the Turks but his force was routed at the Battle of Manzikert. Romanos was captured by Arslan and allowed to go free but a crueller fate awaited him on his return to Constantinople where he was deposed, blinded and exiled.

Urban saw a great opportunity for the papacy in the Turkish threat. In reality, he had little interest in helping the Byzantines as success would merely benefit Byzantium. Instead, his focus was on gaining a victory that would ensure the Pope's status as the true leader of Christendom. Speaking from a throne raised on a dais below the church of Notre Dame du Port in Clermont, the Pope addressed a large crowd of bishops, knights and commoners. Robert the Monk recorded how he exhorted Europeans to take up arms and wrest the Holy Land from what he described as a 'wicked race':

> ... this land which you inhabit, shut in on all sides by the seas and surrounded by the mountain peaks, is too narrow for your large population; nor does it abound in wealth; and it furnishes scarcely food enough for its cultivators. Hence it is that you murder one another, that you wage war, and that frequently you perish by mutual wounds. Let therefore hatred depart from among you, let your quarrels end, let wars cease, and let all dissensions and controversies slumber. Enter upon the road to the Holy Sepulchre; wrest that land from the wicked race, and subject it to yourselves... God has conferred upon you above all nations great glory in arms. Accordingly undertake this journey for the remission of your sins, with the assurance of the imperishable glory of the Kingdom of Heaven.

Thus were the Crusades born, a series of invasions of various parts of the Holy Land, by different people and countries and for different reasons, which continued until 1270.

The People's Crusade

Urban planned that the First Crusade would begin on the Feast of the Assumption, 15 August 1096. Such had been the power of his oratory, however, that a number of excursions to the Holy Land were undertaken in advance, the most notable – known as the People's Crusade – led by a charismatic priest from Amiens known as Peter the Hermit. 40,000 Crusaders, mainly untrained fighters and including many women and children, left for the Holy Land. The Turks massacred them when they got to Anatolia.

The First Crusade

Later in 1096, the First Crusade proper left for Jerusalem, led by a mixture of French knights and Norman nobles, including Robert of Normandy, older brother of William II of England. This far more organised venture enjoyed success. They took a number of cities such as Antioch and Edessa and eventually captured the biggest prize of all – Jerusalem – murdering just about every inhabitant, Muslim, Jew and even Christian. If the Byzantine Emperor, Alexius, thought the recaptured lands would be returned to him, he was to be disappointed. The Crusaders established four new Crusader states in the territory they named 'Outremer' (Over the Sea). These were the County of Edessa, the Principality of Antioch, the County of Tripoli and the Kingdom of Jerusalem. Godfrey of Bouillon, Duke of Lower Lorraine (c. 1060–1100), became Jerusalem's first ruler, although, rather modestly, he did not style himself 'King'.

The Second Crusade

After the fall of the city of Edessa to the Turks in 1144, Pope Eugene III (Pope 1145–53) commissioned the Cistercian abbot, Bernard of Clairvaux, to preach a Second Crusade (1145–47) to the Holy Land. It was a two-pronged attack. The Pope authorised one part of the force to take on the Moors who had occupied much of the Iberian Peninsula since around 710. This effort became part of the *Reconquista*, the recapture of the peninsula from the Moors that would go on until 1492. It successfully attacked Lisbon and gained other territories from the occupying force.

Meanwhile, in the east, the Crusaders unaccountably ignored their original target of Edessa and proceeded to Jerusalem which was not actually under any threat. With 50,000 troops, they also launched an unsuccessful attack on the friendly city of Damascus. Things went from bad to worse. Nur ad-Din, King of Mosul (ruled 1146–74), who had easily defeated the Crusaders at Damascus, conquered Syria. In 1149, he defeated and killed Raymond, Count of Antioch, one of the main Christian leaders in Outremer, sending his severed head to the Caliph of Baghdad as a present. Jerusalem would fall into Muslim hands again in 1187, when Sultan Saladin (ruled 1174–93) routed the Crusaders at the Battle of Hattin.

The Third Crusade

With Saladin installed in Jerusalem, Henry II of England (ruled 1154–89) and Philip II of France (ruled 1180–1223) buried their differences and decided to launch another invasion of the Holy Land. Henry's death meant that the new king, Richard I 'The Lionheart' (ruled 1189–99) was at the head of the English forces. The elderly Holy Roman Emperor, Frederick I Barbarossa (ruled 1155–90), added his massive army to the crusading force, but died before reaching the Holy Land, drowning in a river in southeastern Anatolia.

The force enjoyed some initial military success and captured Acre but arguments over the division of spoils and a mutual distrust led King Philip and Leopold V of Austria (1157–94), who had taken over from Frederick, to return home with their armies. Richard defeated Saladin at the Battle of Arsuf but lacked the resources to take Jerusalem. He concluded a truce with Saladin and set out in October 1192 for England where he was needed. On his way home he was captured by his old rival, Leopold, and handed over to the Holy Roman Emperor, Henry VI (ruled 1191–97). Richard was imprisoned until a ransom was paid and he was released on 4 February 1194.

The Fourth Crusade

There was little heart for another crusade and, when Pope Innocent III (Pope 1198–1216) pressed for one, European monarchs took little notice. Nonetheless an army was assembled, under the leadership of the Italian Count, Boniface of Montferrat (1150–1207). The original objective was Egypt but the Crusaders made little attempt to travel there. Instead they destroyed the Christian city of Constantinople, massacring its population after Alexius IV Angelus (who ruled briefly in 1203–4) reneged on the promises he had made of rich rewards if they helped him to overthrow his uncle, Emperor Alexius III Angelus (ruled 1195–1203). The Crusaders established a Latin Empire in Constantinople and put Baldwin of Flanders (ruled 1204–5) on its throne. Latin rule over large parts of the Byzantine Empire lasted until 1261. Almost none of the Crusaders actually made it to the Holy Land.

The Fifth, Sixth, Seventh and Eighth Crusades
The next four Crusades – in 1216, 1228, 1248 and 1270, respectively – all ended in failure, falling victim to a range of catastrophes – plague, drowning and military incompetence. By the end of the thirteenth century, the powerful military caste of the Mamelukes of Egypt ruled the Muslim world. Their recapture of Acre in 1291 signalled the end for the Christians in the Holy Land. The Crusades were over.

Kings and Kingdoms

As Europe readied itself to welcome in the fourteenth century, it still did not come close to resembling the Europe we know today. Indeed, the first stirrings of the modern European nation states would not begin until late in the coming century and Europe was still made up of countless lordships and small, local power bases.

France, for instance, was controlled by a number of parties. A large part of the country, stretching from Brittany to Aquitaine, came under the power of the English throne because, since William the Conqueror, the Dukes of Normandy had been vassals of the English king. The land to the east of the Rhône, known as Burgundy, was part of the Holy Roman Empire and therefore in German hands. Meanwhile, to the south, Provence was governed by the counts of Catalonia and Barcelona, also kings of the Iberian state of Aragon.

The thirteenth century brought some important changes to the geopolitical make-up of the continent. The French King Philip Augustus (ruled 1182–1223) regained sovereignty over Brittany, Normandy, Anjou and Aquitaine and reclaimed authority over the counties of Champagne and Flanders when, at the Battle of Bouvines in 1214, his army decisively defeated an alliance orchestrated by England's King John (ruled 1199–1216) and consisting of John, Otto IV of Germany (ruled 1198–1215) and Count Ferrand of Flanders (1188–1233). Not only did John lose all the English fiefs in France, he had to go home to face his rebellious barons. He was forced to sign the *Magna Carta*, a cornerstone of British common law and one of the most historically significant documents of all time.

The Iberian Peninsula was a mosaic of kingdoms, Portugal having gained independence in 1139. The southern part of the peninsula had been occupied by the Muslims – or Moors – since 711 and was known to them as Al-Andalus. In 1212, a major turning point in the peninsula's history occurred when a Christian coalition consisting of King Alfonso VIII of Castile (ruled 1158–1214), Sancho VII of Navarre (ruled 1194–1234), Pedro II of Aragon (ruled 1196–1213) and Afonso II of Portugal (ruled 1212–23) defeated the Muslim Almohad army at the Battle of Las Navas de Tolosa. It was a victory that hastened the decline of Moorish influence in the Iberian Peninsula and provided encouragement for the centuries-long *Reconquista*, the reconquest of the lands held by the Moors. Eventually, it would lead to the expulsion of the last Moors in 1492, when Queen Isabella of Castile (ruled 1474–1504) and her husband, King Ferdinand II of Aragon (ruled 1479–1516) began the centralisation of royal power and, hence, the process of unifying Spain. For its part, in 1252, Portugal became the first country to establish its present-day borders when King Afonso III (ruled 1248–79) drove the Moors out of the Algarve.

Gothic Art

It is often the case that the terms used to name art movements are insulting, rather than descriptive. So it was with Gothic art, reputedly named thus by the artist Raphael who had a profound loathing for the style. Raphael, of course, as a great Renaissance painter, was a committed classicist and saw the Gothic style as the work of descendants of the Goths, barbarians who had destroyed his beloved Roman civilisation. It was not until the nineteenth century that there was a reappraisal of Gothic art and the term became respectable and, although inaccurate, purely descriptive.

The progenitor of the Gothic style was a patron rather than an artist. Abbot Suger (c.1081–1151) was a French abbot-statesman – one of the last of this hybrid – as well as a great historian and confidant of the French kings, Louis VI (ruled 1108–37) and Louis VII (ruled 1137–80). In 1122, he became the abbot of the Parisian church of St Denis. For Suger, the new style was *lux continua* ('unbroken light'), seen to some extent already at Monte Cassino in Italy and in the glorious windows of Canterbury Cathedral. He began applying the principles in evidence in these buildings to the old church of St Denis, which had been consecrated in 775 by none other than Charlemagne himself. The work took from 1135 until 1144 and was carried out by artisans from the Low Countries and craftsmen from Italy, specially imported for the task at great expense. The transformation was incredible. On the western side, a new monumental façade was introduced, highlighted by beautifully sculpted doors made of bronze. Rich mosaics added colour to the interior and high, ribbed vaulting drew the eye heavenwards. Most striking of all were the 14 tall stained glass windows, splashing coloured light into the church's interior, recounting the holy story in vibrant imagery and highlighting the magnificent, bejewelled altar.

Until then, the Romanesque style of architecture (known in England as 'Norman') had prevailed, an imitation of Roman architecture with rounded arches. The pointed arch of the

Gothic style, however, had many advantages over the rounded version. Different widths could be spanned much more easily and flying buttresses could be used to support the walls, enabling architects to create walls of inspirational glass, with a rose window as the main highlight. The Gothic style soon spread from its Parisian birthplace and worshippers across Christendom were being offered pictures of Biblical events. In painting and sculpture, the Gothic style first appeared around 50 years after the completion of St Denis. Increasingly applied to arches, stained glass and illuminated manuscripts, it was characterised by a more naturalistic approach to imagery and was representative of a more prosperous and ordered society than had existed several hundred years previously. In the fourteenth century, it took on a much more refined and delicate aspect, seen by some as mannered, and evolving into the style known as International Gothic. This, in turn, would lead to the dazzling achievements of the Renaissance.

Heresies and Social Unrest

At the beginning of the fourteenth century, a combination of factors led to a series of revolts and general unrest in Europe. People had become tired of the systemic corruption that existed amongst the ruling classes and in the Church. Added to this were the problems created by the rush of people from the countryside to the towns and cities where they believed there were richer pickings and a way of life that was less demanding than living off the land. However, rents were high and getting higher, as were prices, and the labour market was heavily over-subscribed. Those who were fortunate enough to find work were dismayed to find that the cost of living was far outstripping wages. Furthermore, taxes rose on a royal whim.

In the countryside, it was, if anything, even worse and many peasants were forced to become beggars. Lawlessness was rife. The gap between rich and poor was growing dangerously wide, creating a tension that was ready to erupt at any moment in violent revolt. In northern France it led to the uprising known as the 'Jacquerie', after the habit of nicknaming any French peasant 'Jacques' from the padded surplices known as *jacques* which they tended to wear. In 1356, the French king, John II the Good, was captured by the English at the Battle of Poitiers. In his absence, the government of France was taken over by the States General, King Charles II the Bad of Navarre (ruled 1349–87) and John's son, the Dauphin. They were dangerously divided, however, and disputes led to serious disunity. The nobles, merchants and clergy, fearful for their lands, wealth and rights, began to charge the peasants ever-increasing taxes, creating dissatisfaction and anger, especially since many of the peasants believed that the defeat at Poitiers had been partly due to the corruption of the nobles. The problems were exacerbated by grain shortages and the ever-present threat of a famine such as the Great Famine that had decimated Europe from 1315 to 1317.

Rebellion finally erupted in 1358 in a series of horrifically violent and bloody revolts. A contemporary account – *The Chronicles of Jean le Bel* – describes the full horror of the events of that year:

> [The peasants] killed a knight, put him on a spit, and roasted him with his wife and children looking on. After ten or twelve of them raped the lady, they wished to force feed them the roasted flesh of their father and husband and made them then die by a miserable death.

There was little organisation, however, and the revolts were soon brought to an end when the leader, Guillaume Cale (?-1358), was captured and decapitated.

In spite of the failure and loss of life in the Jacquerie revolts, similar expressions of public disgust occurred in other places. Rebellious peasants rose up in the cities of Béziers, Rouen and Montpellier and, between 1381 and 1384, the group known as the Tuchins, armed gangs of peasants and craftsmen, revolted against tax levies and the presence of mercenaries who robbed and killed at will without any interference from those in charge. In Florence, workers seized the government of the city; in Flanders there were uprisings; Catalonia experienced a revolt against the nobility; and in England, in 1381, Wat Tyler (1341–81) famously led a march by discontented peasants on London which ended in his death and the deaths of his associates.

Hundreds of years of misdeeds by the clergy also placed the Church in the firing line during the thirteenth and fourteenth centuries. Some people, wishing to return to a purer form of religion, called for church reform, debating the status of the clergy and the right of the people to preach the gospel. The Waldensians were an example of this type of heresy, believing in apostolic poverty as the way to salvation. Pope Lucius III had declared them heretics in 1184 and they were persecuted for several centuries to come.

Others had begun to develop alternative systems of worship but, in 1199, these heresies had been declared by Pope Innocent III to be treason against God. The principal targets of his anger were the Cathars, or Albigensians, a religious sect in the Languedoc in southwestern France. The Cathars were spiritual descendants of the Gnostic Manichaeans who emerged in Persia in the third century and who believed that good and evil were two divine principles. They practised vegetarianism, believed in the equality of men and women and supported a caste of *perfecti* – the spiritual elite and true core of the movement. The murder of a papal legate returning from the Languedoc gave Innocent the excuse for which he had been looking. He called for a Crusade against the Cathars on the same terms as were promised in the Crusades against Islam – remission of sins and unrestricted looting.

The bloody Albigensian Crusade was launched in 1209 and lasted for 20 years. It seems not to have mattered whether people were Cathars or not. When the Cistercian abbot-commander, Arnaud-Amaury, was asked how the troops would be able to tell the difference between Catholic and Cathar, he is said to have replied chillingly, 'Kill them all; the Lord will recognise his own.' When the city of Béziers was attacked in 1209, 20,000 Cathars were massacred. The Church was ruthless in its treatment of these dissidents but they did have the lasting effect of forcing it to adjust to the rapid changes that were taking place in society.

The Black Death

The Middle Ages drew to a close with the resounding crescendo of the Black Death, one of the deadliest pandemics in history. It killed an estimated 50 million Europeans, between 30 and 50 per cent of the population of the continent. Having arrived in Europe in the 1340s, it returned in 1360, 1369 and 1374. It would not really go away until the 1700s, returning with wearying regularity and with varying degrees of virulence every generation.

There are several theories as to the origins of bubonic plague, but it is widely believed that it is carried in the stomachs of fleas that infest rats. It probably first appeared in China and was brought to Europe by Genoese sailors who arrived at the port of Messina on 13 October 1347. Once in Italy, it quickly spread in a northwesterly direction, striking France, Spain, Portugal and England by the middle of 1348. Between 1348 and 1350, it ravaged Germany and Scandinavia, eventually arriving in north-western Russia in 1351.

There are also numerous theories for its cause. One such theory claims that it appeared because the continent had, quite simply, become overpopulated; the new developments in agriculture meant that people were living longer. The English philosopher, Thomas Malthus, writing at the end of the eighteenth century, put forward the theory that human beings could reproduce too quickly and their numbers could outgrow the food supply. The population had, indeed, risen in the previous two centuries, from 50 million in 1315 to 73 million in 1350, in spite of famine and other epidemics such as smallpox and influenza. Whatever the cause, the social upheaval was immense and the impact on society was immeasurable.

The population loss led to profound economic and demographic change. The sudden shortage of labour gave power to the peasants and landlords were forced to compete for their services. Wages went up and freedoms were offered in exchange for work, improving the lot of peasants enormously. Workers became more mobile and no longer had to rely on long-term contracts, moving around from one highly paid temporary job to another. Fewer people also meant more fertile land, leading to cheaper prices for land and more food for everyone. Consumption of meat and dairy products increased and countries such as Germany and the Scandinavian nations began to export their beef and butter. All of these developments would have a beneficial long-term effect, with a significant rise in population just over a century after the plague. Of course, much of the change was not to the liking of the upper classes who made every effort to introduce wage control and to keep earnings at a pre-plague level. These efforts met with varying degrees of success, sometimes leading to the kind of social unrest that characterised much of the fourteenth century.

There is little doubt that the horrors of the plague led four-teenth-century people to rethink their lives. Death had become an all-too-familiar, everyday part of existence and things could never really be the same again. Within a few years a cultural movement was spreading its ideas across western Europe almost as fast as the plague pandemic. The world was about to experience an intellectual transformation, with great developments in science, art, education and countless other fields. The sometimes glorious, but more often violent, Middle Ages were about to give way to the brilliance of a new age – the Renaissance.

Rebirth

From Crisis to Renaissance in the Fourteenth and Fifteenth Centuries

In the 1300s, Europe had evolved rapidly. The Holy Roman Empire was no longer the all-pervasive power that it had been since the days of Otto I. It was losing out to the local interests of the German principalities and the Emperor – who, it should be remembered, was elected to his throne – no longer wielded the power that the position had brought in the past. This had implications for the whole of Europe where change was also very much in the air.

In Italy, for instance, which would become the heart of the Renaissance, prosperity and cultural innovation were the staples and power had devolved to city officials. However, the cities remained individual entities – city-states – competing against each other for trade and wealth. Conurbations such as Genoa, Venice, Florence and Milan were ruled in the fourteenth and fifteenth centuries by powerful families. The Doge of Venice was elected annually but, inevitably, he always came from the ranks of one of the city's wealthy families and did not wield that much power. His city, however, would reach the zenith of its power and influence in the fifteenth century, gaining territories, including Padua, on the Italian mainland.

Florence was ruled by a group of feuding families known as

the *signoria*. In 1433, Cosimo de' Medici (1389–1464), who had been effectively ruling the city without ever being elected to public office, was expelled by jealous rivals. The following year, he returned and seized power, controlling it for the remainder of his life. Milan was governed from 1395 to 1447 by 12 successive members of the Visconti family, who made their head the Duke of Milan. This was followed by the rule of five members of the wealthy Sforza family, who conquered Milan in 1450 and made it one of the leading cities of the Italian Renaissance, governing until 1499. Rome would flower once again in the fifteenth century under the enlightened papacy of the Florentine Nicholas V (Pope 1447–55).

Across the Mediterranean to the west, the Iberian Peninsula moved ever closer to unification. Aragon, Barcelona and Valencia were linked in a federation and they were also tied with Sicily in Italy's south. When Aragon also took Naples, Sardinia and Corsica, it gained dominance over the entire western Mediterranean, laying the foundations for the great seafaring nation that the unified Spain was about to become. Unification arrived in 1469 with the marriage of the two powers of Castile and Aragon in the shape of Isabella of Castile and Ferdinand of Aragon. All that remained was the 1492 eviction of the Moors from Grenada, their last foothold in this part of the world, and Spain was one.

France and England, on the other hand, had been at war with one another on and off since 1337. The Hundred Years War actually lasted longer than a hundred years, only coming to an end in 1453 when the French recaptured Bordeaux, leaving the port of Calais as the English king's only possession in France. It was a different kind of war and, involving as it did other countries from across the continent (Aragon, Castile, Scotland and Burgundy all took sides), it provided a model for future conflicts. It arose out of the feudal issue of vassalage. Since William the Conqueror, Duke of Normandy, the kings of England had remained vassals of the king of France. As they had gained land in France, largely through marriage, they had been reluctant to pay the French king the homage he was due. So the series of battles took place that made up the war and French nationalism became enshrined in the body of a nineteen-year-old woman – Joan of Arc, the 'Maid of Orléans' (c. 1412–31).

There were cataclysmic changes, too, in the north. In 1397, Queen Margaret of Norway (ruled 1388–1412) succeeded in uniting the crowns of the Scandinavian monarchies into the Kalmar Union that would last, intermittently, until 1523. To the dismay of the Slavs, Eastern Europe had been gradually Germanised since the twelfth century, as Germans had migrated to the vast empty territories of the east. This was coupled with the warlike Teutonic Knights' conquest of Prussia. In the face of these irritants and the threat of Mongol invasion from the east, the Czechs and the Poles began to organise themselves into independent states, with religious thinker and philosopher, Jan Hus, playing a large part in the development of Czech nationalism.

Meanwhile, the Poles had become increasingly concerned by the Teutonic Knights' envious glances at Lithuania. In 1386, Poland and Lithuania became linked when Grand Duke Jagiello of Lithuania (ruled 1386–1434) married Hedwig, a Polish princess. Jagiello became king of both countries and, at the Battle of Tannenberg in 1410, he decisively defeated the Teutonic Knights, securing the fledgling Polish state and ending the power of the Teutonic order once and for all.

In the thirteenth century, the Mongols had conquered Russia and it had become no more than a tributary state of the Golden Horde. In 1327, Ivan I of Moscow moved the country's capital from Kiev to Moscow and the Mongol hold on the country began to decrease following their defeat by Grand Prince Dmitri Donskoy at the Battle of Kulikovo in 1380. Further south, the once great power of Byzantium had long faded and now it faced the growing threat of the Turks to the east. They had created the Ottoman Empire, named for their leader Osman I (ruled 1299–1326), and were now moving into eastern Europe where they would dominate for many centuries. In 1453, Constantinople's defences were breached by Sultan Mehmet II's cannon and he entered the city. A thousand years after the fall of the Roman Empire in the West, the Eastern Empire, last vestige of that great imperial power, fell.

From Feudalism to the Modern State

In the feudal system that had prevailed for so long, the king had been at the top of a pyramid of power. Beneath him were countless smaller powers, each dependent on the one above. At the bottom of the heap, of course, was the lowly peasant. There was a gradual evolution of this system as the fourteenth century arrived, the Roman notion of 'the common good' becoming popular and kings becoming more interested in the good of the people as a whole, rather than in just serving their own interests and those of their nobles. Rather than being identified by their position in the hierarchy of power, people were now located in a social grouping, known as an 'estate'. Generally speaking, there were three groupings – the nobility, the clergy and the commoners. This last grouping could be further split into a number of sections – the burghers or urban middle class (a new phenomenon) and the peasants.

In this early form of modern society, therefore, people were no longer defined by wealth or power but by their function and by corporate institutions and, the clergy excepted, heredity became the key factor in deciding to which estate an individual belonged. The nobility's military function and ownership of land ensured that, despite the growth of standing armies, their role was still vital, and they often governed the countryside through regional assemblies which administered justice. It was, however, becoming increasingly difficult for the part-time gentleman soldier to carry out his duties as before. Armies needed proper training and a body of professional military officers began to emerge. The estate of the burghers was controlled by the freedoms and rights of the self-governing cities and especially of the city guilds, associations of craftsmen. There was also a division between these free men and the vast majority of people who owned no property.

Increasingly, these estates would meet to govern and make decisions regarding taxes and so on. No longer were countries governed purely on the whim of a monarch. He often had to take the estates' wishes into consideration and had to seek their authority for tax increases. A charter of rights was sometimes created to protect the rights of the people. Thus, although the king increasingly became the central figure in a country, absolutism was avoided, as is evident in France in the fifteenth century where the embryonic modern state first began to appear during the reign of Louis XI (ruled 1461–1483). In the Holy Roman Empire, an assembly known as the Imperial Diet – the Reichstag – had been meeting informally for centuries; it, too, began to gain power at the expense of the emperor.

The creation of geographically defined nation states eroded the power of the papacy that had reigned supreme for so long. People no longer united behind the Pope, but behind their king, feeling united by their ability as a group to withstand attack from another country or people. National governments increased their authority with the appointment of civil servants, drawn often from the bourgeoisie. Permanent standing armies also encouraged the centralisation of power. Rich merchants, unwilling to see a change in the status quo, made substantial loans to the crown to ensure that outside threats could be dealt with, either by a well-equipped army or by the hiring of mercenaries.

The Western Schism

The Gascon, Bertrand le Got, became Pope as Clement V in 1305 and, four years later, relocated the papacy to Avignon on grounds of security – Rome was dangerously unstable. The Avignon Papacy would last until 1377 and, during that time of seven French popes and a French-dominated College of Cardinals, Christendom was divided. Some countries rejected the authority of the Avignon popes.

Widespread discontent in the Church manifested itself sometimes in a retreat into mysticism or sometimes in downright dissent. Dissent and discussion of Church reform were, of course, ill-advised, given the threat of the Inquisition, the institution created by the Catholic Church to suppress heresy, a task which it performed with ruthless enthusiasm. Nonetheless, men such as the Englishman, John Wycliffe (c.1330–84) and the Czech, Jan Hus (c.1372–1415), were severely critical of many elements of the Church, from its wealth to the concept of papal supremacy. Hus was burned to death for his beliefs and Wycliffe's already-buried body was exhumed in 1428 and burned.

Gregory XI (Pope 1370–78) returned the papacy to Rome but, when he died shortly after doing so, the Avignon papacy's reputation for corruption and French influence led to riots, with Romans demanding a Roman pope. Since no suitable candidate was available, the cardinals elected the Neapolitan Urban VI (Pope 1378–89) but, regretting their decision, shortly afterwards elected another pope – the so-called antipope Clement VII – and relocated the papacy once again to Avignon. Never before had an antipope been elected by the same College of Cardinals as had elected the legitimate pope and, to make matters worse, they elected a third pope in 1409 when neither of the rivals turned up at a council convened to reconcile their differences. The diplomatic crisis that followed divided Europe.

Only in 1414 did the schism come to an end when the reformist conciliar movement won the day at the Council of Constance. Summoned by the German king, Sigismund of Luxembourg, 29 cardinals, 100 'learned doctors of law and divinity', 134 abbots and 183 bishops and archbishops converged on the small lakeside town of Constance in Switzerland. The cardinals deposed all three popes and elected Odo Colonna as Martin V (Pope 1417–31). Instead of embarking on a programme of reform, however, he immediately published confirmation of all the decisions made by his predecessors.

The Renaissance

The term 'Renaissance', meaning 'rebirth', as a description of the period from the fourteenth to the sixteenth century, was first used in 1855 by the French historian Jules Michelet. Although it is a term whose meaning is widely understood, it is, nonetheless, difficult to define precisely. What is certain, however, is that it describes a period of remarkable achievement in a great many fields, from art to science, philosophy to poetry and theology to music. In a letter to Paul of Middleburg, the humanist philosopher Marsilio Ficino wrote in 1492:

If we are to call any age golden, it is beyond doubt that age which brings forth golden talents in different places. That such is true of this our age [no one] will hardly doubt. For this century, like a golden age, has restored to light the liberal arts, which were almost extinct; grammar, poetry, rhetoric, painting, sculpture, architecture, music, the ancient singing of songs to the Orphic lyre, and all this in Florence. Achieving what had been honoured among the ancients, but almost forgotten since, the age has joined wisdom with eloquence, and prudence with the military art... it has recalled the Platonic teaching from darkness into light...

For the nineteenth-century Swiss art historian, Jacob Burckhardt, the fourteenth and fifteenth centuries saw the birth of modern man. That may be largely true, but, if the Renaissance did one thing, it was to place mankind firmly centre stage. Instead of being merely God's playthings, victims of the snakes and ladders of misfortune, people now felt the desire to analyse and understand how the universe worked and, by so doing, to establish some control over their fate.

The Renaissance cultivated a revival of learning derived from classical sources. Thinkers scoured monastic libraries for obscure classical texts, writers began to use the vernacular in their work and this, in combination with Johannes Gutenberg's invention of the printing press in Mainz in Germany in 1440, made books available and accessible to many more people. There was a fascination with classical art because it managed to reproduce the beauty of the human form three-dimensionally. The classical statue of *Laocoön and His Sons* being dragged under water by a sea serpent would be unearthed in 1506 and significantly influence Italian Renaissance art. Moreover, the fall of Constantinople in 1453 brought an influx of Greek scholars to Florence. These experts introduced the Florentines to Aristotle and Plato and the philosophy of Neoplatonism was created to merge Plato's ideas with Christian teachings.

Although it is impossible to say exactly when the Renaissance began, many pinpoint the poetry and songs of the Italian scholar Petrarch (1304–74) as the starting point. Petrarch, a master of the sonnet form in poetry, was one of the earliest humanists. His work often deals with real people with personalities and human emotions, a striking change from literature that had gone before. Giovanni Boccaccio (1313–75), meanwhile, wrote the *Decameron*, a collection of stories of people living during the Black Death that satirised the Church, priests and religious belief. What was different about his writing was that it dealt with people's responses to the plague and not God's reason for inflicting it on people.

In art, painters such as Cimabue (c. 1240–c. 1302) and Giotto (c. 1267–1337) pioneered a new approach to artistic representation, eschewing the formal, stiff, Byzantine style and turning, instead, to nature for inspiration. Giotto, in particular, created figures that had solidity and the scenes he depicted were filled with passion and imagination. The great sixteenth-century art biographer, Giorgio Vasari (1511–74) wrote of him:

> He made a decisive break with the... Byzantine style, and brought to life the great art of painting as we know it today, introducing the technique of drawing accurately from life, which had been neglected for more than two hundred years. (Giorgio Vasari, *Lives of the Artists*, trans. George Bull, Penguin Classics, 1965)

Pioneers in other fields included the great architect Filippo Brunelleschi (1377–1446), who created the magnificent dome of Florence Cathedral, the sculptor Donatello (c. 1386–1466), the most influential artist of the fifteenth century, whose naturalistic statue of *David* created a sensation, and the political philosopher Niccolo Machiavelli (1469–1527), whose cynical view of power and politics, as expounded in works such as *The Prince*, has remained contentious ever since.

People began to think more about their lives on earth rather than their spiritual life and the afterlife. Humanists like Gianozzo Manetti could assert 'the genius of man... the unique and extraordinary ability of the human mind'. The humanist approach to life and learning is characterised by this mode of thought, and amongst its exponents were political philosophers such as Thomas More (1478–1535) who depicted a perfect society created by Christian humanist ideals in his novel *Utopia*. Humanist theologians like the Dutchman Erasmus (1466–1536) and the German Martin Luther (1483–1546) seriously challenged current religious thinking and practice.

The Peace of Lodi in 1454 brought a forty-year hiatus in the fighting between Milan, Florence and Naples. Other Italian states joined them in an Italian League designed to keep foreigners out and the stability, prosperity and peacefulness of the period encouraged the writers and artists alive and working during this time to achieve great things.

Art

The development of linear perspective in painting was one of the most important elements of Renaissance art. Giotto, working in the thirteenth and fourteenth centuries, was amongst the first to take an interest in the technique of creating a representation of realistic distance, using devices and arranging his figures in a manner that often make his paintings resemble stage sets. However, the real credit for perspective went to Brunelleschi who invented the *Construzione Legittima* that formalised the rules of perspective. The analysis of light and shadow and, in the case of Leonardo da Vinci (1452–1519), human anatomy, added to the trend for more realistic painting. Amongst the artists who wielded most influence were Leonardo, Michelangelo (1475–1564) and Raphael (1483–1520).

In the north, too, there was a flowering of the representational arts and the paintings of Dutch artists Hugo van der Goes (c. 1440–83) and Jan van Eyck (c. 1395–1441) even influenced some of the Italian masters. Van Eyck's use of oils was so innovative and striking that it led Vasari, wrongly, to credit him with the invention of oil painting. The Dutch brought a refreshing naturalism to their work that was appreciated and assimilated by their fellow artists. Elsewhere, talented artists such as painter and printmaker, Albrecht Dürer (1471–1528), working in Germany, also explored the techniques and aesthetics developed first in Italy.

Architecture

Renaissance architecture was very much influenced by the remains of classical buildings, with Roman columns often being used. Technique was also enhanced by developments in the science of mathematics. Furthermore, the discovery in 1414 of *De Architectura*, a book on architecture by the first century BCE Roman architect, Vitruvius, provided Renaissance practitioners with technical knowledge that had been lost for many centuries.

Filippo Brunelleschi was one of the greatest of all Renaissance architects. The dome of Florence Cathedral, completed in 1436, was a technical marvel that drew on the construction techniques used for the dome of the Pantheon in Rome, built in 125 CE. In general, the architecture of the Renaissance displayed an emphasis on symmetry, proportion, geometry and a formal regularity that can be found in works of classical antiquity, especially in those of Rome. Its precepts quickly spread to other parts of Europe.

Science

The Renaissance brought significant developments in many fields of science and the way the universe was viewed. Amongst the most important of these was the focus on empirical evidence to provide proof of theories and discoveries. Coupled with this was the rediscovery of ancient texts, accelerated by the influx into Western Europe of many Byzantine scholars following the fall of Constantinople. Furthermore, the invention of printing made many scientific texts and theories more widely available. Nicholas Copernicus (1473–1543) benefited from the availability of material and sensationally postulated that the earth revolves around the sun and not vice-versa. Some decades later his book containing the theory, *De Revolutionibus*, was placed on the Vatican's list of banned books.

The Northern Renaissance

The French were the first to pick up on what had been going on in Italy. They brought back the ideas and innovations of the Italian Renaissance after Charles VIII's (ruled 1483–98) invasion of Italy in 1494. Francis I (1515–47) is considered to be France's first Renaissance monarch and he was responsible for bringing Leonardo to France where the great artist spent his last years. The influence of the Renaissance can be felt in the works of great writers such as François Rabelais (c. 1494–1553), Pierre de Ronsard (1524–85) and Michel de Montaigne (1533–92). By the sixteenth century, the Renaissance had spread to the Low Countries, Germany and, in the late sixteenth century, to Scandinavia, Central Europe and England. In England it was marked by some of literature's greatest exponents – dramatists William Shakespeare (1564–1616) and Christopher Marlowe (1564–93) and the poet Edmund Spenser. Composers such as Thomas Tallis (1505–85), John Taverner (c. 1490–1545) and William Byrd (c. 1540–1623) also espoused the spirit of the age. Meanwhile, in the Iberian Peninsula, the novelist Miguel de Cervantes (1547–1616) and playwright Lope de Vega (c. 1562–1635) were working.

The High Renaissance

Renaissance art reached its highpoint in the extraordinary period known as the High Renaissance which began towards the end of the fifteenth century and lasted well into the sixteenth. This period saw an explosion of creative genius characterised by the work of such masters as Leonardo, Michelangelo, Raphael, Tintoretto (1518–94), Titian (1485–1576) and Veronese (1528–88). Never before had such technical accomplishment, rich imagination and mastery of composition come together in such a brilliant and controlled way.

Many of the artists had learned their art in Florence in a remarkable, simultaneous flowering of extraordinary talent, but the activities of the fanatical Dominican monk, Girolamo Savonarola, in that city persuaded many artists and writers to flee. Savonarola led a moral crusade in which he burned books and destroyed paintings that he considered immoral. In 1497, he supervised what became known as 'the bonfire of the vanities', the burning of a huge number of works of art and other items that he considered contrary to his moral code. Savonarola's heyday, however, was short. In the following year, he was excommunicated and executed. Florentine-trained artists, many of them driven into exile during Savonarola's brief reign of terror, plied their craft in other parts of Italy, especially in Rome where a series of ambitious and high-spending popes provided many opportunities. Sadly, by about 1525, the great art of the High Renaissance was becoming a thing of the past as it evolved into the sophisticated, but less ground-breaking style known as Mannerism.

The Age of Discovery

Possibly the most dramatic change to the world in the centuries following the medieval period was the discovery of new lands during the so-called Age of Discovery. This would alter everything – people's prosperity, their very view of the world and their relation to it; even their eating habits.

Europeans had already developed a taste for the exotic. The Orient had long been known and visited and Europeans developed a hunger for its untold wealth, its jewels, its precious metals and its spices. Stories spread of the fantastic people and creatures that inhabited distant lands, in particular the legend of Prester John, a Christian patriarch and king who supposedly ruled a fabulously wealthy nation somewhere in the Orient. The tales of the Venetian, Marco Polo (1254–1324), who, at the end of the thirteenth century, had visited the court of the Mongol emperor, Kublai Khan (ruled 1260–71), had become a fourteenth century bestseller.

The first explorers of the new age were Spanish and Portuguese or were sailing under their flags. Men such as Bartolomeu Diaz (c. 1450–1500), Christopher Columbus (1451–1506), Vasco da Gama (1460 or 1469–1524) and Ferdinand Magellan (1480–1521) set out on fantastic voyages of discovery that opened the world to all and brought phenomenal wealth to them, their masters and, ultimately, much of Europe.

The changes in society – the migration from the countryside to the towns, the growth of the population and an economic crisis that had blighted the fourteenth century – all made it necessary for Europeans to look elsewhere for their requirements. Greater productivity and a sizeable increase in farmland would help to put meat and vegetables on the European table. Sugar and spices had also become necessities, as had the need to find a source of the precious metals that paid for everything. As ever, religion was also a factor; the Catholic Church was always in the market for more souls to be saved and the New World was teeming with people ripe for conversion.

Portugal was first into the fray. It was Prince Henry the Navigator (1394–1460), third son of King John I (ruled 1385–1453), who launched the Portuguese programme of exploration. He firstly persuaded his father in 1415 to invade and conquer the Muslim port of Ceuta on the coast of North Africa. The objectives were both strategic and financial. Ceuta guarded the Straits of Gibraltar across the Mediterranean from the Iberian Peninsula, but it was also the lucrative terminus for the Saharan trade routes. Henry's fascination with Africa led to voyages of exploration along the Mauretanian coast that also netted African slaves and goods. He employed cartographers and established a maritime academy at Sagres that taught navigation and was important in the development of shipbuilding technology and instrumentation.

Undoubtedly the most important development was the Portuguese creation of two new ship designs – the carrack and the caravel. The carrack was the first real ocean-going ship in Europe. With its high, rounded stern, an aftcastle and a fore-castle, it was roomy enough to store provisions for long voyages and to provide quarters for the comfort of the crew. Caravels had the advantage over carracks of being smaller and more manoeuvrable, much more suitable for precision sailing along coasts in uncharted waters. Between 1418 and 1425, the Portuguese occupied the Madeiran archipelago and, in 1427, the Azores, which had been known in the fourteenth century but were rediscovered by one of Henry's ships. They were colonised in the 1430s. In 1434, one of his sailors, Gil Eanes, took his ship close to the end of the known world, passing Cape Bojador, a headland on the West African coast. Before long, Henry's ships had passed the southern edge of the Sahara, rendering the trade route redundant, and began shipping slaves and gold back home. In 1490, thirty years after Henry's death, Bartolomeu Diaz reached the Cape of Good Hope and it became possible to circumnavigate the continent of Africa. Eight years later, Vasco da Gama captained the first ship to sail from Portugal to India, a remarkable achievement and one that promised prosperity for Portugal.

Meanwhile, in Spain, a sailor of Genoese origin was making plans to set sail across the Atlantic to find a route to Asia. In 1492, after 61 days at sea, Christopher Columbus made landfall on the island of Guanahani in the Bahamas archipelago. He also visited Cuba, which he believed to be a promontory of Cathay (China), and Haiti. The Vikings had travelled to North America almost five centuries previously, but Columbus's achievement was still outstanding and he was welcomed home with the promise of further missions – in 1498 and 1504 – that led to the enduring Spanish influence on Latin America.

The ambitions of the two Iberian nations inevitably led to conflicts. These were resolved, however, by a papal intervention in 1493. In his papal bull, *Inter Caetera* ('Among Other Works'), Pope Alexander VI divided the New World between Spain and Portugal. Spain was allocated all the lands west of a line 370 leagues west of the Azores; it gave them most of America, excluding Brazil. The Portuguese, meanwhile, got Africa, India and the East Indies. Soon, African slaves were being transported to Brazil to work on the sugar plantations. In the end, Portugal proved unable to develop its territories and, in 1580, when the King of Spain, Philip II (ruled 1556–98), inherited the Portuguese throne, the Portuguese Empire went into decline.

The rivals to Spanish global domination were now England, France and the Netherlands and they set no store by Alexander's division of the world, establishing trading posts at the expense of the Portuguese in the east. The French and the English had long been exploring North America. In 1497, the Italian explorer, John Cabot (c. 1450–c. 1498), sailing under an English flag, was the first European to land in North America, at Cape Breton, Nova Scotia. Like Columbus he was under the misapprehension that he had actually reached China. The Italian Giovanni da Verrazzano (c. 1485–c. 1528), funded by the French crown, was the first European to land on the east coast of the modern-day United States. Cabot and others sought, in vain, a Northwest Passage to Asia that would open up the Atlantic to trade from the east and provide a fast route home. In 1522, ships in the expedition originally commanded by the Portuguese captain, Ferdinand Magellan, completed the first circumnavigation of the world. By the early seventeenth century, European ships could sail to the furthest corners of the earth.

The age of discovery was virtually over. Nonetheless, its impact was far-reaching. European colonial powers had now divided up much of the world between them and, in doing so, they destroyed civilisations and committed genocide, so great was their hunger for slaves, trade and the pursuit of imperial ambitions. They imported diseases never before suffered and, in North America in particular, disease is believed to have killed 50–90 per cent of the indigenous population. Europe, in turn, imported syphilis, but its effects were nowhere near as devastating as those that travelled in the other direction.

International trade exploded. By 1600, 200 ships a year arrived back in Seville from the New World bringing untold wealth in gold and silver. The southerly route around Cape Horn was plied by the Portuguese and then by the Dutch. From the east came Polish grain to feed the growing populations of western cities. Meanwhile, the English were supplying cloth to the Low Countries and English trading companies such as the Muscovy Company (1555), the Levant Company (1581) and the East India Company (1600) began making fortunes for their founders. In the Netherlands, too, the Dutch East India Company, founded in 1602, was trading successfully. In the same year it was established, the world's first stock exchange opened in Amsterdam.

Europe now welcomed a variety of new foods and products – pepper, coffee, cocoa, sugar and tobacco. Tomatoes, potatoes, maize and haricot beans also arrived from the Americas. Trade became global. In Africa, slaves were obtained in exchange for goods made in Europe; the slaves were sold to American plantations and the ships, returning to Europe, carried such items as tobacco, sugar and cotton. Global trade, in turn, brought the birth of capitalism. The banking system was developed and encouraged by trading associations and branches of the most important firms opened in all of Europe's major cities. Credit became available and such techniques as double-entry book-keeping were introduced. Banks began to extend credit to kings and princes who, as a result, interfered more in running their economies, increasingly centralising them.

As a result of the new wealth engendered by global trade, the European economy went through a serious crisis in the sixteenth century. Prices rose by more than 300 percent as a result of the increase in the money supply due to the gold and silver pouring in from Africa and the Americas. The standard of living rose but Europe, not for the last time, began to live beyond its means. The biggest loser was Spain which fell from the grandeur of the sixteenth century to the status of a second-rate power a hundred years later. As untold wealth flowed into the country from overseas, it failed to modernise its industry and squandered its riches. The aristocracy was content to buy luxury items from the rest of Europe, allowing its international rivals to benefit from its wealth. In the seventeenth century, Spain and Portugal entered a severe depression.

Charles V

Charles V (who ruled the Spanish realms from 1516 to 1556) inherited a vast empire that, when he abdicated in 1556, two years before his death, measured some four million square kilometres. Born in 1500, son of Philip I the Handsome, King of Castile (ruled 1478–1506) and Joanna the Mad (1479–1555), he was the heir to four of Europe's leading dynasties – the Habsburgs of Austria, the Valois of Burgundy, the Trastamara of Castile and the House of Aragon. In addition, he would rule over concessions in Africa, in Italy (Sicily, Naples and Sardinia) and immense colonial tracts in the Americas. In 1530, he also became Holy Roman Emperor, succeeding his grandfather, Maximilian I (ruled 1508–19). Charles spent a large part of his reign tussling with the French over the rich but politically unstable Italy. It was a struggle that would continue sporadically for the next 150 years.

However, the real threat to Europe at the time was from the Ottoman Turks. Since Sultan Mehmet II had secured Constantinople for the Ottoman Empire in 1453, they had made advances into Europe. Thrace, Bulgaria, Serbia, Greece and Albania had all fallen to them. They took Belgrade in 1521 and, by the middle of that decade, were close to Vienna, posing a danger to the Holy Roman Empire itself. Meanwhile, they had rallied Muslim troops into threatening Spain once more from North Africa.

Charles believed the only solution to the Turkish threat was a 'Universal Concord' amongst European states. He believed that Christian sovereigns had a duty to stop fighting each other so that they could unite against the Ottomans. He famously gave a speech in Spanish on the subject in front of Pope Paul III. It was never going to happen, especially if the French king, Francis I, had anything to do with it. Francis and Charles went to war again. In 1521, following Francis' capture after defeat at the Battle of Pavia, he was coerced into signing the Treaty of Madrid in which he surrendered to the Emperor the duchies of Milan and Burgundy.

The Pope, Clement VII (Pope 1523–34), meanwhile, led the Italian states against the Empire in a series of inconclusive battles that ended in the Peace of Cambrai in 1529. Burgundy was handed back to the French and Spanish supremacy in Italy was recognised. Further wars followed. But, soon, other matters began to demand the attention of Charles and his fellow monarchs. Not only was there the advance of the Turks to worry them but there was also the rise of Protestantism in France and Germany in the religious revolution known as the Reformation.

Reformation Europe

Religious Revolt

On 31 October 1517, the German monk, theologian and university professor, Martin Luther, pinned a notice containing *95 Theses* on the door of the Castle Church in Wittenberg. Church doors were often used as notice boards and the one at the Castle Church provided a very efficient way of getting information to everyone in the university. Luther's notice, however, was meant for a far bigger audience. Within months it had launched a religious revolution that changed Europe forever.

In 1516, Johann Tetzel (1465–1519), a Dominican friar, was sent to Germany by the Pope to raise money for the construction of St Peter's Basilica in Rome by selling indulgences. Indulgences were, effectively, forgiveness for sins and their sale had become one of the Catholic Church's biggest abuses. However, selling indulgences was just one of many abuses that had become everyday practice amongst the clergy and such malfeasance went all the way to the top. Nepotism was rife in the Vatican and friends and relatives of the pope, whoever he was, were routinely appointed to positions for which they were unworthy. Even out in the parishes, priests were neglecting their duties. These abuses were coupled with growing religious discontent, following the Church's inability to do anything about the famine, war and pestilence that had bedevilled Europe in the last 200 years.

Dissenters such as John Wycliffe and Jan Hus and theologians such as Erasmus, with their new, humanist values, had been unable to bring about change. Pope Julius II (Pope 1503–13) had promised reform when he was elected and eventually called the Fifth Lateran Council – but it failed to make any changes. It ended in 1517, by which time Julius had died and been replaced as pope by Leo X (Pope 1513–21). This was the very year that Luther nailed his *95 Theses* to the church door. By this time, Germany was ripe for religious change. The Pope was extremely unpopular, having just levied a tax, and the emperor had been weakened by bickering with the princes and cities that had elected him. The peasants looked on in disgust as the clergy enjoyed a life of luxury, land-ownership and wealth.

Martin Luther, who had become a professor at Wittenberg University in 1512, was the catalyst. He loathed the practice of selling indulgences and was horrified by Johann Tetzel's claim that 'As soon as the coin in the coffer rings, the soul from purgatory springs' (Bainton, Roland, *Here I Stand: A Life of Martin Luther*. New York: Penguin, 1995, p 60) and had finally resolved to take action. His *95 Theses* contained the seeds of the revolutionary teachings that were to change Christianity forever. Luther believed (or came to believe) that only faith can bring righteousness; the Holy Scripture is the only source of faith; the only worthwhile sacraments are baptism and the Eucharist, or Holy Communion; that the worship of the Virgin Mary and the Saints should be abolished; that purgatory does not exist; that there is no need for priests to be celibate and that monastic and religious orders have no real function. The *95 Theses* were swiftly translated from Latin to German, printed and distributed, and within two weeks Germany was seething with religious discontent. Within two months, his thoughts were spurring debate throughout Europe.

In Germany, the unrest erupted into violence in 1522 when the knights sided with Luther and attacked the Archbishop of Trier. Then, in 1524, the peasants rose up against the lords. On both occasions Luther condemned the rebels. Gradually, however, the princes of the empire converted to Lutheranism, mainly to weaken the Emperor still further but also so they could get their hands on valuable Church property. In 1531 they formed an alliance, the Schmalkadic League. Emperor Charles V was, in the meantime, largely preoccupied with fighting the French. Once peace had broken out between the two neigh-bours, however, he faced up to his recalcitrant princes and, with the support of the pope, defeated them in April 1547 at the Battle of Mühlberg, reconverting around 30 German cities as a result. A year later, with the French now supporting the Lutheran princes, Charles signed the Peace of Augsburg after he was defeated at Innsbruck. It brought peace for 60 years, but the princes gained an important right – *cuius regio, eius religio* ('what-ever religion the prince is, will be the religion of his people'). As for Charles, he was exhausted. He abdicated, living the remainder of his life in a Spanish monastery.

Similar doctrines to those of Luther had been preached and advocated in other parts of Europe. Swiss theologian Ulrich Zwingli (1484–1531) preached Church reform, claiming that the Bible was open to interpretation and denying that the Church should be the ultimate authority. He criticised Church corruption and railed against many other issues, including celibacy, fasting during Lent and the use of images. In 1523, his reforms were taken up by the city of Zurich which became a theocracy and Basle and Berne also began to adopt his theories. The other Catholic cantons of Switzerland opposed these reforms, however, and declared war on Zurich. Zwingli died in the Battle of Kappel in 1531.

Meanwhile, in Denmark and Norway, King Christian III (ruled 1534–59) imposed Lutheranism on his people with the help of the German towns who were members of the trading alliance, the Hanseatic League. In Sweden, King Gustavus Vasa (ruled 1523–60) similarly introduced Lutheranism and made himself head of the Swedish Church. In other countries such as France and Scotland, the ideas of another fiery Protestant were gaining currency. John Calvin (1509–64) was a Frenchman who was forced to flee his country in 1533 because of his reforming ideas. He eventually arrived in Geneva where his thinking was imposed upon the city's governance. Geneva became a theocracy; strict morality was imposed and all worldly pleasures were banned. Those who failed to follow his orthodoxy were persecuted and punished. Pastors were taught Calvinism at the University of Geneva and they spread it across Europe. It was followed in England, France, Bohemia, Poland, Hungary and the Low Countries. John Knox founded the Presbyterian Church in Scotland in 1561, based on Calvinist principles.

In England, church reform grew out of the personal proclivities of King Henry VIII (ruled 1509–47). He wished to divorce his wife, Catherine of Aragon, to marry Ann Boleyn. Pope Clement VII (Pope 1523–34) denied him the divorce but the king pronounced himself divorced anyway in 1533 and married Ann. The Pope excommunicated him, declaring the divorce illegal and the marriage to Ann null and void. The crisis mounted as the papal nuncio was withdrawn from England and diplomatic relations were broken off between England and Rome. In 1534, the Ecclesiastical Appointments Act ensured that bishops could only be appointed that had been nominated by the King. That same year, the Act of Supremacy made the sovereign the head of the Church of England and it became punishable by death to oppose this view. Henry dissolved the monasteries, confiscating all their possessions and opposition was ruthlessly suppressed, as his former Lord Chancellor, Sir Thomas More, discovered when he was beheaded for refusing to sign the Act of Supremacy.

Henry's son, Edward VI (ruled 1546–53) introduced Calvinism, but when Queen Mary (ruled 1553–58), daughter of Henry VIII and Catherine of Aragon, assumed the throne on Edward's death, she bloodily restored Catholicism as the religion of England. The Reformation returned under Elizabeth I (ruled 1558–1603). Five years after she ascended the throne, the defining statements of Anglican doctrine were laid out in the *39 Articles*. Opposition to the Anglican Church included the English Calvinists who would become known as Puritans. Animosity between them and the crown would eventually erupt in the English Civil War.

The Counter-Reformation

The Catholic response to Protestantism, known as the Counter-Reformation, lasted from the reign of Pope Pius IV, around 1560, until the end of the Thirty Years' War in 1648. The surge of Protestantism through Europe was undoubtedly the greatest threat the Catholic Church had ever encountered and, after a period of paralysis when little was done actively to reform the Church, it finally reacted during the pontificate of Pope Paul III (1534–49). Paul was a flagrant nepotist but he also distinguished himself by providing the artists Michelangelo and Titian with some of their most lavish commissions. He recognised the extent of the problems facing the Church and took action, convening one of the most important councils in the history of the Roman Catholic Church, at Trent, in northern Italy.

Reformist Catholics and humanists such as Erasmus had been calling for such a council since Luther's *95 Theses* and Charles V had called for one in 1524. Successive popes had refused to countenance such a meeting, however, fearful perhaps of the erosion of papal authority that it might bring. Meanwhile, to suppress heresy, the Inquisition was reorganised and the Congregation of the Index was set up to censor written works and to maintain a list of banned books. Meeting in 25 sessions in three periods between 1545 and 1563, the Council of Trent, the last ecumenical council for 300 years, introduced major reforms, condemned heresies and defined the Catholic position on many contentious areas such as Scripture, Original Sin, Justification, Sacraments, the Eucharist in Holy Mass and the veneration of saints. It defined modern Catholicism and delivered a direct response to Protestant issues, leaving the implementation of its decisions to the Pope. Consequently, in 1566, he published a *Roman Catechism*, designed to expound Catholic doctrine and to improve the priests' theological understanding. 1568 saw the release of a revised *Roman Breviary*, a book of prayers to be said daily. Then, in 1570, a revised *Roman Missal* became available. This contained the text of the Mass to be said in Catholic churches.

Protestantism was also countered by the establishment of new religious orders such as the Capuchins, Ursulines, Theatines, Discalced Carmelites and the Barnabites. Chief amongst these, however, was the Society of Jesuits, founded in Paris in 1534 by a Basque monk, Ignatius de Loyola (1491–1556). Before deciding to devote his life to God, Loyola had seen service as a soldier and he brought a military discipline to the Jesuits. The order he founded would become one of the Catholic Church's most important weapons in the fight against the new heresy. Jesuits displayed unstinting loyalty to the Pope and opened colleges across Europe, fulfilling their mission to convert heathens, reconvert lapsed Catholics and educate. Above all, they engendered fear amongst Catholics and Protestants alike, a fear derived from their belief that the end justified the means.

Mystics added a spiritual dimension to the Catholic resurgence. Teresa of Alva and John of the Cross were Spanish and belonged to the Carmelite order. Teresa's autobiography, *The Life of Teresa of Jesus*, was very influential and John of the Cross has been described by the twentieth-century Catholic writer Thomas Merton as the 'greatest of all mystical theologians'. Other mystics, such as Francis de Sales and Filippo Neri were also active.

So, by the late 1500s, Catholicism had begun to regain ground lost to the wave of Protestantism begun by Luther and eventually, the march of Protestantism was halted. Lutheranism became limited to Scandinavia and Northern Germany and Calvinism was adopted in Switzerland, Holland, Scotland and Western Germany.

The Wars of Religion

Revolt in the Netherlands

Philip II of Spain became the defender of the Catholic cause, putting the immense wealth of the Spanish crown, recently bolstered by the annexation of Portugal, at its disposal. He faced a number of challenges. Calvinism was becoming increasingly popular in the Low Countries, the Moors of southern Spain were rebelling and the Turks had taken Cyprus. He dealt with the Turkish menace with victory at Lepanto as part of a Holy League consisting of Venice, Rome and Spain. England had become a major irritation, attacking Spanish possessions in the Americas and supporting Dutch rebels in the Netherlands. The Protestant Elizabeth I's execution of Catholic Mary Queen of

Scots persuaded him in 1588 to invade England. However, Francis Drake and his fellow English seamen defeated the Spanish Armada and its ships were then destroyed by a storm in the English Channel.

Philip's ruthless suppression of Calvinism in the Netherlands led to a rebellion that began in 1566 and would smoulder for 80 years. When Dutch nobles demanded autonomy and freedom of worship in the Compromise of Breda, Philip instigated reprisals, condemning to death many involved. Crippling taxes only served to increase the hostility of the Dutch towards the Spanish and they rose up under the leadership of William of Nassau, Prince of Orange and Stadtholder of Holland and Zeeland. In 1579, the Low Countries became divided when Philip's new envoy, Alessandro Farnese, united the ten southern Catholic provinces in the Union of Arras. The seven northern provinces responded by creating the Union of Utrecht. In 1588, these would become the Calvinist United Provinces. They achieved independence in 1609 and were recognised by Spain in the Treaty of Westphalia in 1648.

France

Religious divisions in Europe soon erupted in violence and war. In France, Henry II (ruled 1547–59) had died in an accident during a jousting match. His death created a political crisis, with three different parties vying for power – Queen Catherine de' Medici (1519–89), Henry's widow and mother to three future kings of France; the House of Guise, an aristocratic Catholic family, hungry for power and ardently anti-Protestant; and the Protestants, known in France as Huguenots, whose leaders were Admiral Gaspard de Coligny (1519–72) and the Bourbon family, most notably Antoine de Bourbon, King of Navarre (ruled 1555–62) and his brother, Louis I de Bourbon, Prince of Condé

(1530–69). The Bourbons and the Guises were sworn enemies.

The Huguenots made an attempt to abduct King Francis II (ruled 1559–60), but were discovered. When the king died anyway, his ten-year-old brother Charles IX (ruled 1560–74) assumed the throne, with his mother, Catherine, as regent. She tried to steer a careful course between the opposing factions but, when Guise troops massacred Calvinist Huguenots at a church in Champagne, all-out war ensued. In 1563, Francis, Duke of Guise (1519–63) was killed and Catherine negotiated a truce in an effort to end what she feared could be a long and debilitating war.

The peace was short-lived, however, and hostilities broke out once more, following the massacre of a number of priests in Nîmes. This Second War was brought to an unsatisfactory end in 1568. Just six months later the contending parties were at each others' throats again, Catherine and Charles allying themselves in this conflict with the Guise family. By now, the wars were being fought on an international scale. Queen Elizabeth I of England was providing much of the financing for the Huguenot army, indirectly trying to harm King Philip II of Spain who supported the Catholic side. The Catholics had military assistance in the shape of troops from the Papal States and the Grand Duchy of Tuscany. This Third War also ended unsatisfactorily, mainly due to the fact that the French throne could not afford to continue fighting.

The killings of Huguenots continued, the most notable being the massacre of around 10,000 in Paris and the provinces on the eve of St Bartholomew's Day 1572. This led to the Fourth War that ended when Catherine's other son, the Duke of Anjou, was elected as the first King of Poland. The Edict of Boulogne took away many of the rights previously granted to the Huguenots. However, it was not long before they had all taken up arms again. Charles IX died three months after Henry of Anjou had become King of Poland. Henry secretly returned to France and, in 1575, was crowned Henry III (ruled 1574–89), but fighting had already broken out. Henry, trying to placate all sides, granted a number of concessions to the Huguenots but in response the Duke of Guise, with the wholehearted support of Philip of Spain, the Pope, Sixtus V (Pope 1585–90) and the Jesuits, formed a Catholic League with the express purpose of exterminating French Protestants.

The Sixth War (1576–77) saw King Henry forced to rescind most of the concessions he had made to the Protestants and, two years later, a Seventh War yet again ended in stalemate. An Eighth War began, often known as 'the War of the Three Henrys'. In 1588, the Guise army invaded Paris and defeated Henry III. The King retaliated by having Henry, Duke of Guise (1550–88) murdered. Henry III was himself murdered by an insane monk a year later and the heir to the French throne was Henry of Navarre – a Protestant. On assuming the throne, however, Henry IV (ruled 1589–1610) proclaimed that he would renounce Protestantism and become a Catholic. He went on to make peace with Spain and issued the important Edict of Nantes which allowed the Huguenots freedom to worship in certain places.

The Thirty Years' War

The Thirty Years' War (1618–48), a conflict about religion, fought in Germany by mercenary armies, involved most of the European powers and bankrupted a great many of them. It was hugely destructive, killing about 30 per cent of the population of Germany and destroying thousands of castles, villages and towns.

The 1555 Peace of Augsburg, signed by Holy Roman Emperor, Charles V, had been intended to end the conflict between Catholics and Lutherans, allowing Protestants freedom to worship. Unfortunately, it merely represented a temporary halt in hostilities. Religious differences remained great and the spread of Calvinism in Germany added another faith that had no place in the Peace of Augsburg. Moreover, Germany's neighbours had an interest – Spain because the Spanish Netherlands was a close neighbour; France because, caught between the two Habsburg states of Spain and the Holy Roman Empire, she saw an opportunity to take action against the German states and would side with the Protestants in the war. Meanwhile, Sweden and Denmark had long cast hungry glances at the northern German states on the Baltic coastline.

At the beginning of the seventeenth century, the Rhine lands and those south of the Danube were Catholic; those to the north were dominated by Lutherans, with some areas of Calvinist pre-eminence. Tensions persisted until they overflowed in Bohemia in 1618. The Holy Roman Emperor, Matthias (ruled 1612–19), had no heir and his lands would be inherited on his death by his cousin, Archduke Ferdinand II of Austria (ruled 1619–37), who had been elected Crown Prince of Bohemia in 1617. Ferdinand was a fervent Catholic and was very unpopular in Protestant Bohemia which favoured the Elector of the Palatinate, the Calvinist Frederick V (ruled 1619–20). With the support of foreign allies, Bohemia revolted, launching hostilities that would continue for three decades.

Ferdinand solicited help from his nephew, Philip IV of Spain (ruled 1621–65), while the Bohemian nobles applied for membership of the Protestant Union which was led by Frederick V, promising him the throne of Bohemia. Unfortunately, similar offers were made to the Duke of Savoy, the Elector of Saxony

and Prince of Transylvania. When these were made public by the
Austrians, support for Bohemia faltered. The conflict escalated
quickly, fighting breaking out in Lower Austria and Hungary.
Vienna was put to siege by the leading Bohemian nobleman,
Count Thurn (1567–1640) and, in 1619, the Protestants
suffered defeat by imperial troops at the Battle of Sablat. Upper
and Lower Austria signed an alliance with Bohemia in August
1619 and, in that same month, Ferdinand was deposed and
replaced by Frederick. The imperial armies, meanwhile, were
driven out of Hungary. At this point, Spain entered the conflict,
dispatching an army to provide support for the Emperor. They
also persuaded the Saxons to invade Bohemia. The army of the
Catholic League took Lower Austria and defeated Frederick at
the Battle of White Mountain towards the end of 1620, marking
the end of Bohemian independence. It would become Catholic
and remain under Habsburg control for the next three centuries.

The next phase began when the Lutheran Danish king,
Christian IV (ruled 1588–1648), fearful for the independence of
his country following the recent Catholic successes, supported
the Lutheran rulers of Lower Saxony against the imperial forces.
Both France and England helped to fund his initiative and he
formed the Lower Saxon Circle, raising an army of 35,000 men,
amongst them 20,000 mercenaries. However, Christian's allies
let him down. England was weak and divided, France was preoccupied by its own civil war, and Sweden was embroiled in war
with Poland-Lithuania. The fighting ended with the Treaty of
Lübeck in 1629 and Christian had to abandon his support for the
Protestant German states. As a result, the Catholics made more
advances and gained more territory in Germany. The Swedes
were next to make an intervention on the side of the German
Lutherans, under the leadership of their king, Gustavus II
Adolphus (ruled 1611–32). His reasons were similar to those of

his Danish counterpart – fear for the security of his country and its influence in the Baltic states. To begin with, his armies, subsidised by the French, enjoyed great success, regaining much of the territory lost to the Catholics. Gustavus Adolphus was killed at the Battle of Lützen in 1632 and, without his leadership, the Protestants were defeated. In 1635, the Peace of Prague ended this part of the war, but only the Protestant rulers in the northeast were made secure.

Now the French entered the conflict, declaring war on Spain in 1635 and the Holy Roman Empire in 1636. The fighting started off badly for France. Spanish troops invaded from the south and Habsburg forces triumphed in the east, even threatening Paris before they were repulsed. When the prime movers of the war, Cardinal Richelieu and King Louis XIII died in 1642 and 1643 respectively, the French began working to bring it to an end. However, with Swedish support, France now began to win and, following the defeats of the imperial army at the Battles of Zusmarshausen and Lens, only the imperial territories of Austria remained in Habsburg possession. French victories led to the Peace of Westphalia, ending both the Thirty Years' War and the Eighty Years' War in the Netherlands.

The power of the Holy Roman Empire was limited as a result of the war and Germany was split into numerous states that enjoyed sovereignty, despite their membership of the Empire. Spain was also weakened. During the conflict, the Portuguese had ended 60 years of personal union with Spain when they elected John IV of Braganza as king in 1640. The Spanish also lost control of the Netherlands, having to accept the independence of the Dutch Republic in the Treaty of Westphalia. France, meanwhile, became the dominant force in Europe.

The importance of the Treaty of Westphalia in the history of Europe cannot be overestimated. Apart from establishing the boundaries for many of the participants in the war, it set the ground-rules for the modern nation state, changing forever the relationship between subject and ruler. Citizens of a country were now subject to the laws of their own national government. The last great European religious war was over.

Absolute Monarchs

Following the Treaty of Westphalia, France was the most powerful, as well as the most populous, state in Europe. The defeated participants in the Thirty Years' War – Spain and the Holy Roman Empire – were in decline and after years of war and rebellion, the French were hungry for peace and stability. When Cardinal Mazarin, France's First Minister, died in 1661, the young Louis XIV (ruled 1643–1715) decided he would govern alone. Louis would become the embodiment of a new type of ruler, the absolute monarch, whose power is derived directly from God and who embodies the state.

A complex mix of factors led to the rise of the absolute monarch. Following the end of feudal partitioning, power began to be centralised in the monarch, increasing the authority of the state and diminishing the power of the nobles. Further centralisation in the form of standing armies, professional bureaucracies and the acceptance of state laws by all, also contributed.

Louis believed that the king should have total and absolute power and that, ruling by the grace of God, he enjoyed divine right. Thus, everyone and every institution owed obedience to the sovereign – nobles, parliaments, communes and corpora-tions. Responsibilities were devolved to secretaries of state, but the final decisions lay with Louis. He insisted on control of the Church and, despite the fact that the French had fought on the

Protestant side in the Thirty Years' War, he made life very difficult for Protestants in France. As a result, some 200,000 left the
country. Absolutism also affected the arts since, in Louis' mind,
the only purpose of literature and art was to celebrate the
achievements of the king. He spent astronomical sums of money
on this 'official' art, creating vast architectural projects such as
the Palace of Versailles.

A number of other monarchs can also be said to have
espoused the tenets of absolutism, most notably Peter the Great
of Russia (ruled 1682–1725), the Holy Roman Emperor
Leopold I of Austria (ruled 1658–1705), Charles XI (ruled
1660–97) and Charles XII of Sweden (ruled 1697–1718) and
Frederick the Great of Prussia (ruled 1740–86).

Louis XIV and French Expansionism

Under Louis XIV, France's long struggle to curb Habsburg
power in Europe continued for many years and through
numerous wars. In order to protect France and, at the same
time, bask in the glory of conquest, as befitting the 'Sun King',
Louis sought to extend the French frontiers. To do this, he
created a standing army, raising taxes to do so. Commanded by
brilliant generals, it became the best-trained and best-equipped
army in Europe.

In 1665, France invaded the Spanish Netherlands and seven
years later it was the turn of the United Provinces. Meanwhile,
Montbéliard, Colmar, Strasburg, parts of the Saar and
Luxembourg were annexed. The Spanish Habsburgs were unable
to prevent this French expansionism and the Austrian branch was
engaged in fighting off the Turkish threat from the east. Vienna
was saved in 1683 only by the intervention of the Poles, led by
King John III Sobieski (ruled 1674–96). Finally the Turks were

defeated by imperial forces at the Battle of Mohacs in 1687 and the Battle of Zenta in 1697.

By the time war broke out between Louis' troops and the Habsburgs in 1689, Louis' absolutist power in France was waning. The League of Augsburg was formed against the French, consisting of the Catholic Habsburgs of Spain and the Holy Roman Empire, as well as the Protestant nations of England and Holland. The war was brought to a close with the 1697 Treaty of Ryswick which attempted to achieve a compromise that would suit all and establish a balance of power in Europe to prevent further warfare.

Within three years, however, the War of Spanish Succession had broken out between the Holy Roman Empire, Austria, Great Britain, the Dutch Republic, Prussia and Portugal on one side and France, Spain, Hungary and the Electorate of Bavaria on the other. It arose over a dispute about the succession to the Spanish throne by the Bourbon Philip V (ruled 1700–46), Louis XIV's grandson. Fighting was ended by two treaties – the Treaty of Utrecht in 1713 and the Treaty of Rastadt the following year. Philip of Anjou became King Philip V of Spain; Austria gained all of Spain's possessions in Italy – Milan, Naples and Sicily – as well as the Spanish Netherlands; Britain gained Gibraltar, Malta and Minorca in the Mediterranean and Nova Scotia and Newfoundland in Canada, as well as a lucrative agreement to supply Spain's colonies in the Americas with slaves for 30 years. More than 400,000 people had died, but, critically, French power had been curbed in Europe and a balance had been achieved that would bring a welcome period of calm and relative stability.

Great Britain's Two Revolutions

For some monarchs, absolutist ambitions brought dire consequences. In the case of the Stuarts in England and Scotland, they
resulted in revolution, execution and, ultimately, the end of their
dynasty. The crowns of England and Scotland had been united in
1603 on the death of Elizabeth I when the Stuart, James VI of
Scotland, was offered the throne and also became James I of
England. His son, Charles I (ruled 1625–49), made life and
worship very difficult for the Protestants in Scotland and
England – Presbyterians and Puritans, respectively. His ill-
considered attempt to impose the Anglican Prayerbook on the
Scots resulted in them invading England. Then, as he tried to get
Parliament to pay for an army to fight the Scots, they rebelled,
issuing the Grand Remonstrance against him, condemning the
policy that had led to this situation. Bloody civil war broke out
in 1642 and Parliamentary troops, mostly Puritans, led by
Oliver Cromwell (1599–1658), defeated Charles at the Battles
of Marston Moor (1644) and Naseby (1645). Charles I was eventually captured and executed in 1649.

England became a republic for the only time in its history,
with Oliver Cromwell as, effectively, head of state for the next
11 years. From 1653 to 1658, he was officially designated Lord
Protector of England. On Cromwell's death, however, the
Stuarts were restored in the shape of the former king's son,
Charles II (ruled 1660–85). When Charles died, his brother,
James II (ruled 1685–88) rapidly displayed that he had learned
nothing from the problems encountered by their father. Indeed,
he espoused the Catholic cause and even showed signs of wanting
to reign as absolutely. It proved too much for the English who
deposed James in a bloodless coup – the Glorious Revolution –
and offered the throne to the Protestant Dutch aristocrat,

William of Orange (ruled 1689–1702), James's son-in-law. In 1689, William and his wife, Mary (ruled 1689–94), became King and Queen of Great Britain after their acceptance of a Bill of Rights that, amongst other things, made the monarch subservient to the law of the land. Britain's future as a constitutional monarchy was secure and a model was created for the rest of Europe.

Baroque Culture and Science

The conclusions of the Council of Trent had penetrated deep into society. Amongst the areas given special attention by the cardinals were the arts. The brilliance of the High Renaissance. had given way in the sixteenth century to the witty, intellectual style that became known as Mannerism. The Council of Trent, however, called for representational art that could be understood by the uneducated, illiterate masses and not just an educated elite. A generation later, that style, later to be described as 'Baroque', blossomed exuberantly across Europe.

Baroque artists rejected the cool restraint of neoclassicism as displayed in the Renaissance and championed a dramatic and expressive sensuousness. Artistic effects such as *trompe l'oeil* and *chiaroscuro* delighted the viewer as did the grandiose quality of Baroque works of art, whether in the discipline of sculpture, of painting or of architecture. The magnificent naturalism of Caravaggio (1571–1610) or Annibale Carracci (1560–1609) gave painting new impetus for the first time since Raphael with technical innovation and staggering emotional impact. Artists across Europe also developed the style in their own way – Diego Velasquez (1599–1660) in Spain, Pieter Paul Rubens (1577–1640) and Anthony van Dyck (1599–1641) in Antwerp and Rembrandt van Rijn (1606–69) and Jan Vermeer (1632–75) in the Netherlands.

Literature, too, was given new life. In Spain, Miguel de Cervantes (1547–1616) published *Don Quixote*. Meanwhile in England, William Shakespeare (1564–1616), was creating the greatest works in the history of English literature.

Perhaps the most vivid manifestation of Baroque style was in architecture. Dramatically exuberant buildings were built, designed to demonstrate power and control and ultimately to create awe in the eye of the beholder. St Peter's Square in Rome designed by Gian Lorenzo Bernini (1598–1680) and the Piazza Navona by Francesco Borromini (1599–1667) in the same city provide stunningly grandiloquent examples of the architecture of the time and their influence can be seen in buildings across Europe.

The Baroque period also engendered a critical scientific revolution that at last left behind the medieval view of the world. The mathematician, Johann Kepler (1571–1630), developed the groundbreaking heliocentric view of the universe shown in the work of Copernicus, concluding that not only the earth but also the other planets revolved around the sun. The Italian Galileo Galilei (1564–1642) showed that movement obeyed mathematical laws and demonstrated empirically that Copernicus was correct. Isaac Newton (1642–1727), working in England, developed laws of gravitation while William Harvey (1578–1657) made invaluable discoveries about the circulation of the blood. In France, meanwhile, the great thinker, René Descartes (1596–1650), challenged absolutism with his rationalist view of the world, as discussed in his *Discours de la Méthode*. This work is often cited as sowing the seeds for the mode of thinking that would characterise the eighteenth century – the period known as the Enlightenment.

Breaking Free

The Age of Enlightenment

The sheer joy of Baroque art and architecture had provided a little light relief for those who lived in the seventeenth century, for it had been a difficult and dangerous time to be alive. War, famine and pestilence had ravaged Europe, resulting in a population of around 100 million, a headcount that had not changed in a century. Successive poor harvests and a lack of agricultural development did not help and a series of disastrous epidemics – smallpox, typhus and cholera – had a devastating effect. Plague was almost as virulent as in the fourteenth century and, even though the number of babies surviving birth was on the rise, it had been more than offset by the frighteningly high death rate.

Furthermore, the second half of the century had seen Europe in deep recession, as imports of gold to Spain went into decline. Only trade prospered and Great Britain and, especially, the Netherlands were the major beneficiaries, the Channel and North Sea ports becoming the most important in the world. Dutch shipping controlled the Atlantic and Indian Oceans and they dominated the important spice trade through the Dutch East India Company, founded in 1602, creating a large colonial empire in the process. By 1700, the British had overhauled the Dutch to become the world's leading global trader, building an empire of their own and adding 13 colonies along the North American east coast to possessions in Canada and the West Indies. The Bank of England, founded in 1694 by a Scotsman, William Paterson, became the world's most important financial institution and sterling Europe's strongest currency.

Meanwhile, across Europe, affairs were less secure, especially economically. High rents and taxes created poverty and social unrest. The nobility, enriched by the money generated by increased rents, moved to large expensively appointed town houses from their country estates and became courtiers. The rich became richer and the poor became poorer, and angrier. Much of the seventeenth century had been blighted by clashes between lords and peasants, both in the countryside and in towns.

The horrific conflicts and diseases of the seventeenth century may have been long gone, but life was not a lot better in the eighteenth century, especially for the poor. With improvements in medicine and healthcare, the population rose, but there was barely enough food to feed them all. Towns became overcrowded as peasants left the countryside in search of better prospects, only to find appalling living conditions. People began to realise the need for improvements in transportation, roads and safety. Town planners began to create large open spaces, providing recreational opportunities.

The agricultural revolution in the eighteenth century greatly changed farming practices and increased yields, particularly in Britain. Mechanisation, the use of enclosures and four-field crop rotation were introduced and innovators such as Jethro Tull (1674–1741) devised new ideas that helped to feed the increasing population. This increase in population in Britain would eventually provide the workforce necessary to drive the industrial revolution in the late eighteenth and nineteenth centuries.

There were many efforts to help the 'deserving' poor. The Church operated various organisations and in a number of Protestant countries, measures were enacted to raise taxes to aid those in trouble. Hospitals were becoming more numerous but treatment, especially surgery, remained, at best, rudimentary. Anaesthesia was being used more often, however, and the discovery of a smallpox vaccine by English scientist Edward Jenner (1749–1823) represented a huge advance.

Thinkers of the Enlightenment

Men such as René Descartes (1596–1650) and Isaac Newton (1643–1727) had, in the seventeenth century, created a new way of thinking and of describing the world. Descartes began with his famous, '*Cogito, ergo sum*' ('I think, therefore I exist') – you can, with the help of reason and mathematics, prove the existence of God. Other philosophers, such as the Englishmen Thomas Hobbes (1588–1679) and John Locke (1632–1704) and the Frenchman, Blaise Pascal (1623–62) had also questioned the status quo. Most importantly, the Swiss thinker, Jean-Jacques Rousseau (1712–78), took Locke's thinking and built on it. Locke had said that people are born equal and are the sum total of their individual experience and observations. In *The Social Contract* Rousseau claimed that 'Man is born free, but everywhere he is in chains.' He advocated that power should be given to the people. The French philosopher and writer, Voltaire (1694–1778), meanwhile, poured scorn on institutional religion.

It was hardly surprising then, after centuries of religious and political repression and tyranny overlaid with superstition and mysticism, that people began to wish for a society based on Reason. Enlightenment thinkers were severely critical, too, of the repression of individual and personal liberty by political and religious institutions. Such thinking would lead, ultimately, to the American and French Revolutions in the eighteenth century and also contributed to later events such as the Latin American independence movement and the Greek national independence movement, culminating in the Greek War of Independence, fought between 1821 and 1829. Another element of the Enlightenment perhaps arose partly from Europeans' experience of the 'natural' lives lived by the natives of the lands that had been recently discovered. Works such as Benedictus de Spinoza's *Ethics* expounded a pantheistic view of the world with God and nature as one. Nature would become a *leitmotif* of Enlightenment literature.

The Treaty of Utrecht had made Europe a relatively safe place in which to travel and many young men took themselves off on the Grand Tour, buying art and shipping it home and soaking up ideas and styles. Architecture began to reflect the influence of the Grand Tourists and the influence of the Italian architect Andrea Palladio (1508–80) became pervasive. Palladio influenced English architects such as Christopher Wren (1632–1723) and Inigo Jones (1573–1652). Italianate villas began to spring up in the English and Irish countryside. As the eighteenth century progressed, however, romanticism became the fashion. Garden designers such as 'Capability' Brown (1716–83) made natural-looking landscapes *de rigueur* and this taste for nature reverberated through the arts with poets such as William Wordsworth (1770–1850) whose work rejoiced in the natural, unspoilt beauty of England's Lake District. In music, too, romanticism became popular across Europe later in the century.

Enlightened Despots

While most countries were monarchies, the styles of government varied from country to country in Europe at the beginning
of the eighteenth century. Absolutism had taken hold and most
kings or emperors ruled by 'divine right'; they were entitled to
rule by their birth and were responsible for their actions to no
one but God.

However, there were those amongst this ruling elite who
became interested in the new ideas of the Enlightenment and
who tried to apply them to politics, in spite of their absolutism.
They became known as enlightened despots and embraced such
rationalist principles of the Enlightenment as religious tolerance, freedom of speech, freedom of the press and the right to
own property. They allowed and encouraged the development of
science, the arts and education in their countries. In Denmark,
Count Johann von Struensee (1737–72), *de facto* regent while
the schizophrenic Christian VII (1749–1808) was king, tried to
introduce enlightened reforms, freeing the serfs, improving the
legal system and introducing religious tolerance; unfortunately,
his dictatorial style resulted in his downfall and execution. In
Italy, Leopold of Habsburg, Grand Duke of Tuscany, later briefly
Holy Roman Emperor (ruled 1790–92), introduced reforms
including fair trials and the abolition of torture. In Spain, Charles
III (ruled 1759–88) reformed the law and expelled the Jesuits.
In Sweden, King Gustavus III (ruled 1771–92) abolished
torture.

Another enlightened despot was Catherine II of Russia (ruled
1762–96). The Russians had finally broken free from the Mongol
yoke in the fifteenth century with the help of the Orthodox
Church. The Romanovs had come to the Russian throne in 1613
and would remain there until 1917. Peter the Great, Tsar from

1682 until 1725, extended Russia's territory and integrated his nation with the west, improving industry and administration, travelling incognito throughout the west to learn from new developments there. He had introduced the rule that each Tsar had the right to choose his successor and this resulted in a chaotic period in Russian imperial history. Eventually, Peter's grandson, Peter III (ruled 1762), became king. His wife, a German, had changed her name to the more Russian-sounding Catherine and she was a remarkable woman. Fearing her mentally immature husband was going to divorce her and marry his mistress, she had him assassinated in 1762. As Catherine II, she then became Empress of Russia.

She enjoyed a succession of lovers chosen from her imperial guards and she corresponded with French thinkers – notably Voltaire – about how she could apply the principles of reason to the government of Russia. In 1767, she reorganised the Russian legal system along rational lines, using as her inspiration, *L'Esprit des Lois* ('The Spirit of the Laws') by the French Enlightenment social commentator and political thinker, Charles de Montesquieu (1689–1755). She applied his view that prisons should rehabilitate inmates, for example, reducing the number of executions and abolishing torture. While founding schools and defining the privileges that Russian nobility could enjoy, however, she did nothing to change the condition of serfdom in which millions of Russian peasants laboured. The Enlightenment principles of individual liberty and the abolition of slavery did not interest her.

The War of the Austrian Succession

Peace did not last many years in Europe after the Treaty of Utrecht brought the War of the Spanish Succession to a conclusion. In 1740, the Holy Roman Emperor Charles VI (ruled

1711–40) died. He had feared that his daughter Maria Theresa's accession to the Austrian throne would be contested by other European monarchs and nobles. To prevent this, he had persuaded many of them to sign a document known as the *Pragmatic Sanction* which acknowledged their acceptance that the Habsburg lands should be undivided and that Princess Maria Theresa should inherit them all on his death.

Unfortunately, Frederick II the Great of Prussia (ruled 1740–86) was unable to resist the temptation that an inexperienced empress offered and invaded Silesia. Alliances began to form immediately. Spain and France aligned themselves with Prussia. Britain, already at war with Spain, and fearful of France's colonial ambitions in North America and India, opted for the other side and supported Maria Theresa. The war dragged on for eight years before the Treaty of Aix-la-Chapelle brought hostilities to an end. Frederick held on to Silesia and Maria Theresa's husband Francis I (ruled 1745–65) became Holy Roman Emperor, while she ruled in Austria and over the Habsburg lands.

Fighting never really stopped in the colonies, and peace in Europe was again short-lived. In 1756, the Seven Years' War broke out. The alliances had changed and this time, France fought alongside Austria while the British shifted their support to Prussia. In 1763, the Peace of Paris allowed Prussia to retain Silesia. The ultimate winners after these global conflicts were the British who had beaten the French in both the Americas and in India and now reigned supreme in both territories.

Revolutions: America and France

The American Revolution was the first major event to result from the ideas of the Enlightenment. The colonists were engaged in a long-running dispute with their British masters over how much tax they should pay. In 1775, delegates from Britain's 13 colonies met and elected Colonel George Washington as their leader and launched a fight to break British control of the tea trade. A year later, on 4 July 1776, they declared independence from Britain, the Declaration of Independence embodying the principles of the Enlightenment – 'We hold these truths to be self-evident, that all men are created equal, that they are endowed by their Creator with certain inalienable Rights, that among these are Life, Liberty and the pursuit of Happiness.'

France, of course, had supported the American colonists in their struggle against Britain and it had proved a financial burden. However, the king failed to make any reforms to a tax system that was easy on the nobles and clergy and punitive towards the least able to pay – the artisans and the peasants. Poor harvests in 1787 and 1788 exacerbated the problem; wheat prices soared and, consequently, so did the price of bread. Nonetheless, King Louis XVI seemed powerless to improve matters and called a meeting of the Estates General, consisting of representatives of the clergy, the nobility and the Third Estate – the bourgeoisie and peasants. It was the first such meeting since 1614.

As towns and villages across France met to elect their representatives, there was a ferment of debate. This continued at the ensuing meeting, the National Assembly. While the nobles argued for the status quo, the Third Estate argued for reform. Tempers ran high and eventually, on 14 July 1789, a crowd of disgruntled Parisians attacked the Bastille prison in Paris in search of weapons. Unrest escalated throughout the country and many nobles, sensing the direction events were taking, fled the country. On 4 August, the Constituent Assembly abolished the feudal society that had held many peasants in virtual slavery.

Towards the end of that month the Declaration of the Rights of Man and of the Citizen was adopted and, by 1791, France had a written constitution that made Louis a constitutional monarch. Reform was introduced into the Church and the power of the Pope was diminished. When the Royal Family attempted to flee Paris in June 1791, they were captured and returned to the capital. Then, in April 1792, Louis declared war on the other European powers, hoping that victory would restore him to his former status. It was a war that would continue until 1815, long after his death.

The war did not start well for France, many of the army leaders having fled. Then, when Prussia and Austria announced that were they to win, they would restore Louis' full powers, the people of France, already suspicious of their king's loyalties, suspected collusion with the enemy. Further revolutionary activity erupted on 10 August 1792. Louis was deposed and executed the following January, as were many other aristocrats and clergymen in the months to come. In September 1792, France proclaimed itself a republic. Revolutionary fervour served the French army well and it enjoyed a good autumn. It changed the art of warfare, for the first time engaging an entire nation in a war, with conscription and promotion from the ranks instead of by birth. On the execution of the king, however, France's enemies formed an alliance, the First Coalition, comprised of almost all the nations of Europe. They declared war on France.

France's problems multiplied with rebellion and civil war as it tried to raise an army. The National Assembly split into two opposing factions – the Girondins, determined to protect the principles of 1789 – and the Montagnards or Jacobins – more concerned with establishing a dictatorship to protect public safety. Amongst the Montagnards were men such as Jean-Paul

Marat (1743–93), Georges Danton (1759–94) and Maximilien de Robespierre (1758–94). The Montagnards won the day and many of the Girondins faced the guillotine. The Montagnards established a Revolutionary Government and became known for the Terror, a period of extreme violence that lasted from September 1793 until July 1794. Mass executions were carried out across France and around 40,000 people are said to have been guillotined. After the execution of Robespierre himself in 1794, a new constitution was drawn up. The following year, the National Convention, which had come into existence with the proclamation of the Republic, was replaced by two councils – the Council of Elders, consisting of men over 40, and the Council of Five Hundred, an assembly of deputies. Real, executive power was vested in a group of five men known as the Directorate.

By 1799, France was in turmoil again, threatened with invasion by the allied forces of the Second Coalition while the young General Napoleon Bonaparte's expedition to Egypt was stranded following Horatio Nelson's defeat of the French fleet in the battle of the Nile. The threat of a coup persuaded the Directorate to call on Bonaparte to return to safeguard the political institutions. Not only did he safeguard them, he took them over.

Napoleon Bonaparte

Napoleon Bonaparte (1769–1821) was a Corsican who had risen through the ranks at an alarming speed, achieving a number of stunning victories. Under his leadership, France had enjoyed increasing military success, taking Belgium, Nice, Savoy and annexing the left bank of the Rhine. Countries that were occupied became 'sister republics'. Holland became the Batavian

Republic, Milan, the Cisalpine Republic, Genoa, the Ligurian Republic. In 1798, the Helvetic and Roman Republics were established and the following year Naples became the Parthenopean Republic.

Although his Egyptian adventure had not been the success he had hoped for, he was still given a hero's welcome on his return. He was also invited to be part of a coup but, instead, usurped the coup for himself. In November, 1799, the thirty-year-old Napoleon became First Consul, playing the leading part in a ruling triumvirate governing France. In 1802, he was named First Consul for Life and then, in 1804, following overwhelming approval in a plebiscite, he became Emperor, as Napoleon I. France made peace with Austria in 1801 and then Britain in 1802. Napoleon had already made his peace with Rome and the papacy in the Concordat of 1801. Meanwhile, reform continued at home that affirmed many of the revolutionary principles, such as equality before the law.

Peace with Britain foundered after just a year, colonial quarrels setting the two old enemies at each others' throats yet again. Victory at the Battle of Trafalgar (1805) confirmed British naval supremacy and soon the other European powers – Austria, Prussia and Russia – had rejoined the fray against the French. Napoleon enjoyed victory at Austerlitz in 1805, Jena in 1806, Friedland in 1807 and Wagram in 1809, but his lack of naval power was a major drawback. In 1810 and 1811, he was at the zenith of his power. Bonaparte family members ruled Spain, Naples and Westphalia and France controlled vast swathes of Europe. The Holy Roman Empire had been replaced in 1806 by the Confederation of the Rhine, no more than a French satellite state, while Hamburg, Amsterdam, Rome and Brussels were all under French control.

However, the decline had already set in. The Spanish

campaign begun in 1808 was long and arduous, the Spaniards wearing Napoleon's armies down with their guerrilla tactics. His invasion of Russia in 1812 became first a retreat in the face of the harsh Russian winter and then a rout. Germany rebelled in 1813 and, by 1814, France was surrounded and outnumbered. On 6 April, Napoleon abdicated in favour of his son and was exiled to Elba. He remained there until the following year when he famously returned to rule France for another hundred whirlwind days. He was finally defeated by the Duke of Wellington (1769–1852) and the Prussian general, von Blücher (1742–1819), at the Battle of Waterloo on 18 June 1815. His next exile, on the isolated Atlantic island of St Helena, was final.

The Congress of Vienna

The Congress of Vienna – a conference of ambassadors of the victorious Allies – convened in Vienna from November 1814 until June 1815, meeting even during the period when Napoleon returned from Elba, and signing its Final Act eight days before his conclusive defeat at Waterloo. It determined the future shape of Europe.

In France, the Bourbons were restored to the throne, under Louis XVIII (ruled 1814–24), younger brother of the executed Louis XVI, and its borders were reinstated to their pre-Revolutionary positions. Holland was given Belgium, previously under Austrian control. The Allies did not restore the Holy Roman Empire, instead creating the German Confederation, consisting of 39 German states. It was, however, chaired by the Austrian Habsburgs. Prussia, a major force in the Napoleonic Wars, gained the Rhineland and became a major German power. In Italy, the former kingdoms, duchies and principalities were mostly returned to their pre-Napoleonic state. Austria held on to

Lombardy and Venice in the north. Poland virtually disappeared from the map, following its support for Napoleon, most of its territory going to the Russians.

Napoleon's attempt to unite Europe by force had failed and, in so doing, it had betrayed many of the ideas of the Revolution and of the Enlightenment. One of the main reasons for its failure was the new feeling of nationalism that arose in many countries. New ideas of nationhood developed and individual liberty became a hot topic in political debate. Amongst the legacies of the Corsican's rule were the codification of the laws of many countries and a uniform system of weights and measures that has served Europe well ever since.

Europe had been at war since 1792 and it had been ruinous in terms of lives lost and financial cost. In order to prevent it happening again the great powers, led by Lord Castlereagh (1769–1822), the British Foreign Secretary, Metternich (1773–1859), the Chancellor of Austria and Tsar Alexander I of Russia (ruled 1801–25), devised the Concert of Europe, a system of meeting in congress from time to time to resolve problems without resorting to war. It was also a vehicle by which the major powers could crush revolutionary activity before it developed in the way that the French Revolution had. Spain, Naples, Piedmont and Portugal soon experienced the force of this initiative when uprisings in favour of constitutional government were ruthlessly crushed. The British withdrew from the Concert after a short time but the others continued in what was termed a Holy Alliance.

Towards a Modern Europe

Europe in 1800

Following the Napoleonic Wars, the British Empire emerged as the world's leading power. The statistics are staggering; Britain controlled a quarter of the world's population and about a third of its land and sea. Europe still lacked strong nation states, enabling Britain to establish the 'Pax Britannica' around the globe, a period during which it controlled most of the important trade routes and possessed a navy that truly did rule the ocean waves. The period of relative peace it engendered began to weaken as the Europe created by the Congress of Vienna began to fall apart and the Great Powers once again began to make warlike noises.

The Ottoman Empire, which had reigned supreme in Eastern Europe for many centuries, went into decline, raising the spectre of Russian expansionism towards the Mediterranean that ultimately led to the Crimean War (1854–56). The Franco-Prussian War (1870–71) arose out of years of tension between the two countries and was followed by the emergence of the new nation states of Italy and Germany.

Nationalism and liberalism were the two concepts that had the greatest influence on nineteenth-century politics. Borrowed from the French Revolution, they were espoused by the revolutionary leaders of the new century and contributed to the creation of a new Europe. Nationalist tendencies that had become current during the Napoleonic era when, for example, the Russians, the Germans and the Spanish had refused to give in to the French, persuading people to attempt to expel foreign occupiers, and the principles of democracy became aspirations for many liberals. Freedom of speech, freedom of the press and religion were preached while the romantics celebrated heroism and the liberty of the individual.

However, the same old problems of famine, economic stagnation and social inequality persisted and were met with the age-old response of repression. Even in England, aglow with global success, there were demands and, sometimes, violent protests for electoral reform and 11 died in the Peterloo Massacre when thousands protested in Manchester. The Reform Act of 1832 greatly improved the legitimacy of Parliament by increasing the number of men who could vote to 650,000. It contributed to Britain's avoidance of revolution in the nineteenth century.

Repression in Germany took the form of a ban on political meetings, censorship of the press and rigid control of education. In Italy, societies known as the *Carbonari* (charcoal-burners) met in secret to call for the expulsion of all foreign powers and the unification of Italy as a republic. Their rebellions of 1820–21 in Piedmont and, in 1831, in the rest of Italy were easily defeated.

The first major uprising occurred in Greece in 1821. Much of the country had been under Ottoman control since the fourteenth century but Ottoman power was weakening and the time was right for a war of independence. The struggle became an inspiration for European liberals, its romantic standing much enhanced by the death of the English poet, Byron, at the siege of Missolonghi. Britain, France and Russia intervened on the Greek side, destroying the Turkish fleet at the Battle of Navarino, off the west coast of the Peloponnese peninsula, in 1827. Greece finally obtained independence in 1830.

The years 1830–31 saw dissatisfaction erupt into revolution in a number of European countries. In July 1830, Paris rose up once more when the Bourbon monarch, Charles X (ruled 1824–30), made an attempt to remove the constitutional limitations on his sovereignty. He was replaced by Louis-Philippe I (ruled 1830–48), a descendant of Louis XIII. Watching events in France carefully, rebels in a number of other states were stung into action. In Germany, some rulers were persuaded to abdicate and new constitutions were introduced, complete with electoral reform. In Italy, the people of Modena, Parma and the Papal States rebelled against Austrian rule but were swiftly dealt with. A revolt in Poland installed a revolutionary government until the Russian tsar took action in 1831.

The Congress of Vienna had handed Belgium to the Netherlands and, in 1830, the Belgians rose up against the union and their Dutch king. Belgium achieved independence in 1831 but eight years later was at war with its former masters. The 1839 Treaty of London guaranteed Belgian independence and neutrality. Meanwhile, Luxembourg became an independent Grand Duchy, but still within the Dutch kingdom. It would not finally be relieved of Dutch suzerainty until 1890.

Revolution and Rebellion

The lack of success of many of the 1830–31 revolutions and rebellions did little to dispel the feelings of dissatisfaction shared by many of the peoples of Europe. If anything, in fact, these feelings were exacerbated by that age-old cause of social unrest – a series of poor harvests and famines. People were starving again all over Europe.

The century's second and altogether more successful wave of revolution began in Paris, as usual, in February 1848. Louis-Philippe abdicated after fighting against electoral reform. Louis Napoleon Bonaparte (ruled 1848–70), nephew of the Emperor, was elected President of the Second Republic. By 1852 he had disposed of his opponents, often violently, and, following a questionable referendum, in the best Bonaparte tradition he declared himself Emperor as Napoleon III. He would remain in power until 1870 when France lost the disastrous Franco-Prussian War and he was deposed.

Meanwhile, revolution broke out across Europe. In Austria, an uprising by students in Vienna sent their reactionary political leader, Prince Metternich, into exile. The feeble-minded Emperor Ferdinand I agreed to the demands of the people and abdicated. His nephew Franz-Josef (ruled 1848–1916) became Emperor and would reign for 68 years. Following an uprising, King Frederick William IV (ruled 1840–61) of Prussia was forced to grant a constitution and demonstrate his support for a united Germany. A German parliament was elected and it made the decision to declare war on Denmark in order to win back the two German states of Schleswig and Holstein. The matter was unresolved at the end of hostilities and Frederick William impatiently closed the fledgling German parliament. To the east, the Hungarians declared independence from Austria while, to Hungary's annoyance, Croatia immediately declared independence from Hungary. Austria joined in with the Croatians in an invasion of Hungary, but the Russians, fearful of the spread of revolutionary ideas to their own peasants, invaded Hungary and crushed the rebellion.

In Italy, the Italian patriot, Giuseppe Garibaldi, was moderately successful in the First Italian War of independence. Milan had rebelled against Austrian rule and, in Rome, a republic was established, but a French force was sent to bring it down. Eventually, in June 1849, the French prevailed and Garibaldi and his troops retired from Rome to carry on the struggle for Italian freedom elsewhere.

A New Europe

It had been many years since Europe had been at war and, since the end of the Napoleonic Wars, most countries had been looking inwards. By the middle of the century, however, tensions were rising once again. Russia's expansionist ambitions had begun to worry the other European superpowers, although all of them greedily eyed the territories of the fading Ottoman Empire. Eventually the anxieties led to the Crimean War (1854–56), fought between the Russian Empire on one side and France, Great Britain and Sardinia supporting Turkey on the other. The allies won and the Russians were forbidden (by the Treaty of Paris that ended it) from establishing a naval or military presence on the Black Sea coast, a huge disadvantage to them. All the Great Powers promised to respect the independence of the Ottoman Empire.

Germany approached unification, its prime advocate being the great statesman, Otto von Bismarck (1815–98), the Prussian Prime Minister. The Germans defeated the Austrians over the issue of Schleswig and Holstein in 1866, finally driving the Habsburgs from Germany and the unification cause was helped by the outbreak of the Franco-Prussian war in 1870. Prussian victories at Metz and Sedan led to the fall of Napoleon III and the Second Empire. It also led to the final unification of Germany with the Prussian King Wilhelm I (ruled 1861–88) being crowned Emperor.

Defeat for France also hastened unification in Italy. Count

Camillo Cavour (1810–61), Prime Minister of Piedmont, had linked up with the French Emperor Napoleon III in 1858 and driven the Austrians out of Lombardy. Cavour then formed a union with other states in Italy. With his blessing, Garibaldi and a force of *Camicie Rosse* (Red Shirts) overthrew the kingdoms of Sicily and Naples. In 1861, he added Sicily and southern Italy to the new Kingdom of Italy, to be headed by the King of Sardinia, Victor Emmanuel II (ruled 1861–78). Rome was declared the capital of the new state, but Pope Pius IX refused to give up his claim to the Papal States, regarding himself as a prisoner in the Vatican. No Pope would leave the Holy City for the next 59 years.

The Austrians, meanwhile, would focus on creating the dual monarchy of Austria-Hungary. Nonetheless, they still faced the nationalism of the many Slavic peoples under their control – amongst them the Serbs, Montenegrins, Albanians and Bulgarians. Now that the Turks were fading from the picture, these minority peoples, as well as others across Europe, found themselves in states in which they felt like second-class citizens. This sentiment would have dire consequences for Europe and the world in 1914.

A Shift in Population

European economic success led to a massive increase in the population of the continent during the nineteenth century. If Russia is included, it soared from 190 million in 1800 to 420 million by 1900. Fortunately, advances in the nineteenth century in agriculture, transport and industry not only provided the means to feed the growing number of people, but also helped to improve living conditions for many. Public health improvements undoubtedly played a large part. Life expectancy rose dramatically in the developed areas of Europe although in areas such as Eastern Europe harsh living conditions persisted and the death rate remained very high. Migration, too, changed populations as workers moved from the countryside to the towns in search of a better life and many even moved to a different country. Many Irish, for example, crossed to England, looking for work in building the new transport infrastructure as an escape from the disastrous potato famine and ensuing disease in 1845–6.

The new mode of transport, the railway, dramatically changed the way people lived, giving them ready access to travel and allowing the movement of essential commodities. The railways also contributed to the increasing urbanisation of Europe with numerous cities surpassing populations of a million inhabitants. Although many European countries remained staunchly agricultural with a large percentage of the population living in the countryside, Great Britain had the largest urban population with a huge percentage of people living in towns. Nonetheless, large cities across the continent were now becoming massive conurbations – London had 4.7 million inhabitants, Paris 3.6 million and Berlin 2.7 million. Industrialised regions – steel-producing areas such as the Ruhr in Germany or the cotton-producing area of Lancashire in England – also began to attract large numbers of workers. The sleepy village of Essen, at the heart of the Krupp family's steelmaking empire, had a population of 4,000 in 1800. A century later, some 300,000 people lived and worked there. This rapid explosion of towns and cities easily outpaced improvements in living conditions and social problems abounded. People lived in severely overcrowded conditions, without sanitation or access to clean water. The result was disease, death and, to the dismay of those in power, social unrest.

As the century wore on, great advances were made in public

health, and sanitary conditions in many towns and cities improved. In Paris in the 1860s, for instance, French civic planner, Baron Haussmann (1809–91), launched a plan to modernise the city, creating a Paris of wide boulevards. It was no coincidence, in this city of revolutions, that the broad avenues he introduced were too wide for rebels to build barricades across. They certainly contributed to the quick suppression of the Paris Commune that snatched control of the capital for two months in 1871. Provision was also made for an efficient sewage system and water supply. It was a model that would be copied in other cities. Meanwhile, slum clearance programmes were launched in many cities and model towns were built. Many families, however, still lived in sub-standard, overcrowded conditions and they struggled to be able to afford adequate food and clothing.

States introduced measures to alleviate the suffering. The German government made old-age and sickness insurance compulsory and, in the early years of the coming century, Britain set up a retirement scheme. Although such measures were steps in the right direction, they remained inadequate in the face of the huge social problems that rapid industrialisation had brought.

There was some good news, however. Cures and treatments were found for many diseases. Previous killers that contributed to the high rate of infant mortality such as diphtheria, scarlet fever, typhoid and whooping cough, could now be treated. Cholera, a killer of many thousands in London and Paris in the middle of the nineteenth century, had been almost eradicated by 1900. The German physician, Robert Koch (1843–1910), proved that different bacteria caused different diseases and isolated the bacterium that caused tuberculosis. X-Rays were discovered by the German physicist, Wilhelm Röntgen (1845–1923), and the Curies, Pierre (1859–1906) and Marie (1867–1934), discovered radium and radioactivity.

The term 'scientist' was coined in 1833 by the English poly-math and Anglican priest, William Whewell (1794–1866), the need for such a word displaying the growing importance of the new profession of science. There were huge advances in both science and scientific thinking. *The Origin of Species* by the English naturalist, Charles Darwin (1809–82), introduced the concept of evolution by natural selection and stimulated debate on religious, philosophical and scientific grounds that carries on to this day. Frenchman Louis Pasteur (1822–95) was respon-sible for many discoveries in the field of chemistry and the Englishman Michael Faraday (1791–1867) and the Scotsman James Clerk Maxwell (1831–79) significantly changed the science of physics, especially in the fields of electromagnetism and electrochemistry.

The Industrial Revolution

The Industrial Revolution began late in the eighteenth century in Britain and would irrevocably change both Britain and then the rest of Europe as the nineteenth century progressed. Its begin-nings could be traced back to the mechanisation of the English textile industry, with ingenious inventions by men such as Richard Arkwright (1733–92), Samuel Crompton (1753–1827) and James Hargreaves (1720–78). Iron-making tech-niques were improved while the creation of the railways by the English engineer, George Stephenson (1781–1848), and the building of canals provided the infrastructure on which to trans-port the goods that were being produced in Britain's new facto-ries. Vital improvements had been made to the steam engine by Scottish inventor James Watt (1736–1819) and his rotary steam engine was fundamental to the Industrial Revolution, leading to greater machine-based manufacturing and a consequent increase in production capacity. With its phenomenal industrial growth, Britain's output far outstripped that of any other country and 'the workshop of the world', as the country became known, was soon the wealthiest nation on the planet.

Coal and iron-ore were vital to the new technologies and it was in the regions where they were to be found in abundance – a slice of Europe stretching from Wales to the Ukraine, encompassing the Midlands and north of England, northeastern France, Belgium, the Ruhr and Silesia – that industrialisation became concentrated. Belgium was the first place on mainland Europe to reap the benefits of industrialisation, in the coal-mines and iron and zinc factories of Wallonia in particular. With independence in 1831, the Belgian economy grew rapidly. Coal production, for instance, increased threefold between 1830 and 1850. The French textile industry in the northeast of the country also benefited from industrialisation. Linen and silk production flourished and cotton was produced in factories. By 1870, twice as many people were employed in factories as in 1830, while coal and steel production increased by 300 per cent.

In Silesia, the Rhineland and the Ruhr, Germany produced high quality coal and industry began to spread north. Textiles, cotton, iron and coal were produced in the Wupper river valley in North Rhine-Westphalia, while, at Essen, the small steel foundry established by the Krupps in 1811 was, by the 1840s, manufacturing cannons for the Turkish, Prussian and Russian armies. Industrialisation had spread across Europe and made industrial superpowers of Britain, Belgium, Germany, France and Switzerland. Spain, Portugal and southern Italy, meanwhile, had remained largely agricultural. But by the end of the nineteenth century, Britain's economic dominance had begun to wane as Germany overhauled it.

Many other technological advances were made. In the 1890s,

the Italian Guglielmo Marconi (1874–1937) demonstrated wireless telegraphy; in France, following the pioneering work of the Lumière brothers, Auguste (1862–1954) and Louis (1864–1948), the first cinema opened in Paris in 1896; during the second half of the century, various engineers worked on the combustion engine, but it was the Germans, Gottlieb Daimler (1834–1900) and Karl Benz (1844–1929), who became the 'fathers of the automobile'.

Changing Politics

Absolutism had had its day and by 1900, most European countries were governed by monarchies run on constitutional lines or, if they were republics, by presidents. Of course, parliamentary democracy as we know it was still something of a dream. Britain, which had enjoyed a constitutional monarchy since the reign of William III as well as a long-established parliamentary system, probably came closest.

Politics were changing, however, and new political parties were beginning to emerge across Europe as people began to demand a bigger say in the way their country was governed. Karl Marx (1818–83) and Friedrich Engels (1820–95), for instance, published their *Manifesto of the Communist Party* in 1848 and socialism was on the rise throughout Europe. Social Democratic parties, based on the one founded in Germany by August Bebel (1840–1913) in 1875, were founded in a number of countries.

In Britain, activists such as the Scot, Keir Hardie (1856–1915), sought representation for the working class in parliament and, in 1893, the Independent Labour Party held its first conference. It would be another 31 years, however, before the Labour Party would form its first government in the United Kingdom. Workers also began to be represented by trade unions that were legalised across Europe in the later part of the century. They used their power, too. Successful, large-scale strike action was carried out by London dockers in 1889, their victory representing a milestone in the British labour movement. Strike action by coal miners in the Ruhr the same year also emphasised the growing power of the workers. It was a power that did not go unnoticed as governments responded to their calls for better working conditions. Laws were passed everywhere, apart from in Russia and the Balkans, which restricted the length of the working day and introduced safety measures to protect workers. Child labour continued, however.

The changes brought by the Industrial Revolution were probably as great as anything that had ever happened in Europe. They altered the way people looked at the world as much as the new scientific and philosophical developments had shifted people's world-view at the time of the Renaissance. The economic benefits of industrialisation made people more optimistic about the future and the incredible new technologies of the nineteenth century led them to believe in progress and to think that anything was possible. For the first time, people were able to withdraw momentarily from the drudgery of everyday life and indulge in leisure pursuits. Mountaineering became popular and many sports were codified, often by the British. Swimming became popular and the mass production of the bicycle helped to make cycling a popular pastime. The European colonial powers were able to spread their revolution across the world and soon the United States had become a major industrial competitor. Nonetheless, Europe had carved up the world and European culture and values straddled the globe as the nineteenth century drew to a close.

The Descent into Madness

Imperialism

Europeans had good cause for optimism at the start of the twentieth century. Europe, after all, was where the revolutionary technological and scientific discoveries and innovations of the previous century had been made and, although the United States was fast catching up, Europe was at the very heart of things. Wealth poured in, too, from the vast colonial empires that the European superpowers had created, especially in Africa. In 1814, the Congress of Vienna took South Africa from Holland and gave it to Britain. France annexed Algeria after invading in 1830. A year later Tunisia also became a French possession. The Suez Canal opened in 1869 and had attracted a great deal of European attention ever since. In 1882, Britain sent a force to Egypt to put down an anti-European uprising and remained there, much to the annoyance of the French who had been casting hungry glances in that direction for some time. As the 'Scramble for Africa' continued, a conference was held in Berlin in 1884–85 to come to some agreement on the division of the continent. France took most of West Africa; Britain took Kenya in the east and Nigeria in the west; Portugal got Angola and Mozambique; Belgium took the Congo and Germany was given Cameroon, Togo, Tanganyika and Zanzibar.

Of course, the European annexation of Africa spelled disaster for Africans. There was extreme cruelty, as in Belgium's treatment of the Congolese, and violence against men, women and children, as evidenced in Britain's totally unprovoked aggression in the Zulu War of 1879 and attacks on the Ndebele kingdom in Matabeleland in 1893. The British defeated the Boers in South Africa in the Boer War of 1899, but their treatment of their defeated foes – herding them into the world's first concentration camps and burning their crops – excited anti-British feeling across Europe.

Imperial expansion did not stop with Africa. France colonised South East Asia and islands in the Pacific were divided up between them and the other powers. Rivalry between the colonial powers became bitter and, in 1898, Britain and France almost came to blows over the town of Fashoda in the Sudan.

During this period, in spite of the nationalist tendencies displayed in the scramble for territory, important alliances were being formed that would have serious implications for the next century. In 1882, Germany, Austria-Hungary and Italy had formed the Triple Alliance, promising each other mutual support in the event of an attack by any two of the other Great Powers, or, in the case of Germany and Italy, an attack by France. In 1907, Russia, France and Great Britain formed a counterbalance to the Triple Alliance when they put their names to the Triple Entente.

As the new century dawned, Germany and Britain were engaged in a furious arms race, competing with each other to construct the greatest number of battleships and the other powers were not far behind. Twenty-six states met at a Peace Conference in The Hague in 1899 to discuss disarmament, but nothing really came of it, apart from the establishment of the Permanent Court of Arbitration to settle disputes. In 1946 it would become the International Court of Justice. A further conference in 1907 established humane rules for war.

Meanwhile, Europe sizzled with tension and numerous incidents only served to heighten that tension. War twice broke out in the Balkans in 1912–13. The Balkan League, consisting of Bulgaria, Greece, Montenegro and Serbia, conquered Ottoman-held Macedonia, Albania and Thrace in the First Balkan War; the Second Balkan War saw Serbia, Greece and Romania arguing with Bulgaria over the division of the spoils from the first war. Both Austria-Hungary and Germany looked on in alarm as Serbia emerged from these conflicts, its power and status greatly enhanced. War was not far off. It just needed one spark to ignite it.

The First World War

Gavrilo Princip, born in Bosnia-Herzegovina in 1894, provided that spark. In Belgrade to study, he joined the clandestine Serbian nationalist organisation, the Black Hand, a group that sought union between Bosnia-Herzegovina and Serbia and independence from the Austro-Hungarian Empire. On 28 June 1914 he assassinated the heir to the throne of Austria-Hungary, Archduke Franz-Ferdinand and his wife, Sophie, in Sarajevo.

When the government in Vienna demanded that investigators be given complete access to the murder scene, the Serbians replied less than enthusiastically. The Austrians seized the opportunity to declare war, starting a domino effect. Towards the end of July, the Russians, having assured the Serbians of their support, declared war on Austria and Germany. Germany responded by declaring war on Russia and then, at the beginning of August, on Russia's ally, France. When German troops invaded neutral Belgium on 4 August, Britain had no alternative but to enter the fray, declaring war on Germany. Turkey and Bulgaria would add their weight to the Central Powers – Turkey in 1914 and Bulgaria in 1916. In 1915, Italy reneged on its membership of the Triple Alliance and sided with the forces of the Entente, the Allies. In 1917, the United States would rally to the Allied side. The conflict was truly a world war and it proved to be the bloodiest so far in Europe's already bloody history.

The principal theatres were in northern and eastern France and western Russia and it was a war unlike any other that had been fought before. Modern weapons of destruction produced casualties on an unheard-of scale, and a great deal of the fighting was conducted from trenches that faced each other across a few hundred metres of cratered and muddy no-man's land. The weapons were nightmarish and powerful – long-range artillery, poison gas, hand grenades, machine guns, tanks, planes and submarines, not to mention the new battleships, fitted with huge guns. And the casualty numbers resulting from the use of such weaponry were staggering. At Verdun in eastern France, for example, a battle fought from 21 February to 18 December 1916 resulted in more than 250,000 dead and more than a million wounded. At the Battle of Passchendaele, fought between 11 July and 10 November 1917, more than half a million men died.

The war impacted on the civilian population at home, too. Women had to replace men in factories and there were food shortages as German submarines became effective against British merchant ships bringing in supplies. The entry of the United States into the war was decisive and, by autumn 1918, the Germans were retreating and the collapse had begun. Bulgaria surrendered on 29 September, the Turks on 30 October and Austria on 3 November. Meanwhile, in Germany, civil unrest resulted in Kaiser Wilhelm II (ruled 1888–1918) abdicating on 9 November and a republic being declared. The war ended two days later on 11 November. Eight million had died and twice that number had been wounded.

The Russian Revolution

Subject peoples throughout Europe had seized the opportunity provided by the distraction of war to exploit the situation. In 1916, the Irish rebelled against British rule, but were bloodily put down. The southern part of Ireland would have to wait until 1921 to achieve self-determination, the six counties of the north remaining part of the United Kingdom. Meanwhile, Poles, Czechs, Hungarians and Croats all used the gradual weakening of the Central Powers to push for independence.

In Russia, the peasants finally revolted against the draconian rule of the Tsars, in February 1917. Tsar Nicholas II (ruled 1894–1917) abdicated, bringing to an end more than 300 years of Romanov rule. He and his family were shot the following year. The government attempted to establish a republic in place of the monarchy, but Russia remained at war with the Central Powers and conditions worsened with severe food shortages and little success in battle.

In October 1917, the Bolsheviks, who ultimately became the Communist Party of the Soviet Union, grabbed power under the leadership of Vladimir Ilyich Ulyanov (1870–1924), better known as Lenin. A disciple of Marx and Engels, Lenin believed that revolution by the workers could only be possible if they were led by a disciplined, well-organised party. The estates of the wealthy Russian landowners were confiscated and banks and industry nationalised. Anxious to deal with internal matters, Lenin made peace with the Central Powers in March 1918, but for several years the country was ravaged by a bitterly contested civil war, won in the end by the communist Red Army. In 1922 the Union of Soviet Socialist Republics (USSR) was founded with Moscow as its capital.

The Treaty of Versailles: Redrawing the Map of Europe

It was almost impossible to make a peace that would please everyone on the Allied side and not penalise the Central Powers to such an extent that the only possible outcome would be further warfare. While the British wished to re-establish a balance of power in Europe, the French were determined to negate the German threat against them once and for all. US President Woodrow Wilson, on the other hand, aimed at achieving a just peace settlement. His 'Fourteen Points' laid out the major issues and formed the basis of discussion, but were greeted cynically in some places merely as 'Wilson idealism'. Amongst them was the desire to allow people self-determination, the need for disarmament and the establishment of 'A general association of nations... under specific covenants for the purpose of affording mutual guarantees of political independence and territorial integrity to great and small states alike.' This would become the League of Nations, which would meet for the first time in Paris in 1920, just six days after the Treaty of Versailles came into force. Its powers would be limited, however, by the fact that its creator, the United States, never became a member.

With hindsight, a lasting peace for Europe was always likely to be a near-impossibility. After all, it was a peace settlement arrived at by the Allies, with little input from the Central Powers, and resentment burned in German minds for many years at a treaty that was especially punitive to them and appeared to blame them solely for the outbreak of war.

The map of Europe was vastly different at the start of the

1920s to what it had been just a decade previously. Austria-Hungary was no more, the old empire having been torn asunder, and two separate nations, Austria and Hungary, had been established. Poland, having disappeared from the map at another great peace conference, the Congress of Vienna in 1815, was reborn. Romania had declared its neutrality at the outbreak of war but joined in on the Allied side in 1916. Now it was enlarged with the addition of the territories of Bessarabia, Bukovina and Transylvania. A single state, known as the Kingdom of Serbs, Croats and Slovenes was created for the South Slavic people. In 1929, King Alexander I (ruled 1921–34) would rename it Yugoslavia. However, the problems of this part of the world were far from solved by the redrawing of borders. Just as the nations of which it was made up had provided the catalyst for the First World War, they would also be the venue for more violent conflict towards the end of the twentieth century.

Meanwhile, in northern Europe, Finland's autonomy was confirmed. It had been ruled by Sweden from the thirteenth century until the Swedish-Russian War of 1809 when it became a Grand-Duchy within the Russian Empire. Following the October Revolution in Russia and a period of civil war, it had become a republic. Across the Baltic, Estonia, Latvia and Lithuania were granted independence.

Europe remained troubled for some years, despite the Versailles Treaty. In Germany, after the abdication of the Kaiser, the Weimar Republic was established but suffered numerous attempts to overthrow it. Between 1919 and 1921, Poland and Russia fought each other until the Poles confirmed their independent status and their borders with victory. Disarmament seemed to have been forgotten and the proud claims of self-determination for subject peoples often seemed no more than empty rhetoric.

Nationality and Conciliation

The problems of nationality remained prevalent in Europe after the First World War and different nationalities shared countries, sometimes incongruously. Czechoslovakia, for instance, was a racial mélange – Czechs and Slovaks, of course, but also Ukrainians, Poles, Germans and Hungarians. The same could be said of Yugoslavia. The potential for trouble was great and it often flared up over the slightest misunderstanding.

Europe was also in a precarious financial state. The cost of the war had crippled everyone – the victors owed the United States huge amounts that the Americans wanted repaid quickly – and the massive reparations piled on to the defeated Central Powers only served to increase their economic burden and heighten social unrest. The Germans defaulted in their payments in 1923 and the French, ever eager to punish their neighbour to the fullest extent, occupied the Ruhr, supported by the Belgians.

Around this time, the first stirrings of a united Europe could be heard as some suggested that customs barriers served only to impede the transport of goods and harmed industry. The nations of Europe, however, were far from that point. Nonetheless, tensions eased when it was agreed, under American influence, to reduce the reparations that the impoverished Germans should be made to pay. (The Germans would unilaterally stop the payments in 1932.) The French left the Ruhr in 1925 and, in October of that same year, Britain, France, Poland, Italy, Belgium and Germany signed the Locarno Treaties in an attempt to secure the territorial provisions of the Versailles Treaty as well as to normalise relations with the Weimar Republic. Germany became a member of the League of Nations in 1926. Amongst the conciliatory voices of the time was Socialist French Foreign Minister, Aristide Briand (1862–1932), who, in 1930, proposed a federal European union that would establish a 'common market'. But the European states were not yet ready for such a step and it would take another great war and 27 years before his vision would become a reality.

Hitler, Mussolini and the Rise of Dictatorships

In a number of countries across Europe, the vacuum left by the disappearance or weakness of monarchies would be filled by a new political entity – the dictator.

Italy had been disappointed by the post-war settlement and amongst the country's wealthy elite there was also a fear of communism. Many of them threw their weight behind the new Fascist party, led by a squat, bald-headed, former political journalist and soldier, Benito Mussolini (1883–1945). In 1922, Mussolini seized power. Nationalistic propaganda and the preaching of the fascist values of order and discipline as well as the creation of jobs and social programmes, persuaded many Italians that fascism was the right thing for the country, and those who thought differently were soon silenced. Parliamentary democracy was an inevitable casualty and soon like-minded European politicians on the right were casting envious glances at Italy.

In 1929, the United States Stock Exchange collapsed with huge implications for the whole world, but especially Europe with its close business and economic ties with America. As the Depression sank in, it was particularly catastrophic in Germany. By 1932, there were six million German unemployed.

In 1919, a Berlin railway locksmith and poet, Anton Drexler (1884–1942), and six others founded the German Workers' Party. In September that year, Corporal Adolf Hitler (1889–1945), sent to investigate the party by German security services, was invited to join, becoming the party's head of propaganda. By 1933, the

German Workers' Party had become the National Socialist Party and Hitler, promising food and jobs, was Chancellor of Germany. He blamed the Jews, the communists and the Treaty of Versailles for Germany's troubles and immediately set about dismantling the democratic process, calling himself *Der Führer* (Leader) and claiming that he alone could make Germany great once more. The Weimar Republic made way for the Third Reich.

Authoritarian dictatorships appeared in other countries. In Bulgaria, a right-wing faction led by Aleksandar Tsankov (1879–1959) assassinated the democratically elected Prime Minister and seized power; in 1929, the king of the Serbs, Croats and Slovenes, Alexander I, banned political parties and assumed executive power, renaming the country Yugoslavia; in Austria, civil war broke out in 1933 when Chancellor Engelbert Dollfuss (1892–1934) dissolved parliament and established an autocratic regime in imitation of the Italian model; in Poland, the 1935 death of the popular centrist leader, Józef Piłsudski (1867–1935), was followed by authoritarian government; in Portugal in 1932, a military coup installed the pro-Fascist António de Oliveira Salazar (1889–1970) as dictator, a position he would retain for the next 38 years; in Hungary, István Bethlen (1874–1946), a Trans-ylvanian aristocrat, and Miklós Horthy (1868–1957), the extreme right-wing former commander-in-chief of the Austro-Hungarian Navy, ruled from 1920 until 1944, allying with Hitler.

The fight to prevent Spain from becoming a dictatorship became a European *cause célèbre* in 1936 following the revolt of General Francisco Franco (1892–1975) against the incumbent republican government. With arms supplied by the Soviet Union and France, volunteers from many European nations fought in the International Brigades against Franco and his allies, Nazi Germany and Fascist Italy. Half a million lives were lost in a savage war that devastated Spain and presaged the global conflict to follow a few years later. Franco won in 1939 and remained in power until his death in 1975.

Nazi Germany

From the moment in January 1933 that Adolf Hitler was invited to become Chancellor by German President, Paul von Hindenburg (1847–1934), it was obvious to many that his ambitions lay beyond Germany's borders. In his 1925 book, *Mein Kampf*, Hitler had coined the term *Lebensraum* to describe what he believed to be Germany's need for more space. He had also laid forth his hierarchical views on race, placing the German – or Aryan – race at the top of the hierarchy and the Jews at the bottom. His loathing of communism was also made very clear.

In power, the Nazis immediately began a reign of terror, ruthlessly crushing all resistance. The first of the infamous concentration camps, built to torture and imprison opponents of the regime, were constructed in 1933, shortly after an arson attack on the German Reichstag, or parliament. The Nazis used this attack to persuade President von Hindenburg to agree to the introduction of emergency laws to combat the 'ruthless confrontation of the Communist Party of Germany'. The new laws established Germany as a dictatorship. Press, cinema and radio freedoms were withdrawn and civil liberties were suspended. Thousands of communists and other opponents of the Nazis were incarcerated in the new concentration camps.

The greatest victims were the people that Hitler and the Nazis blamed for all of Germany's ills – the Jews. In 1935, the Nuremberg Laws were introduced, severely limiting the freedom of Jews in Germany. They were banned from holding public office, Jewish shops were boycotted and many thousands, fearing for their future in Germany, emigrated. In 1938, on the night of 9–10 November, a pogrom took place across the country, known as *Kristallnacht*. In this one night, at least 92 Jews were murdered and 30,000 were arrested and sent to concentration camps. Meanwhile, synagogues and Jewish cemeteries were attacked. By the end of the forthcoming war, some six million Jews would die in the camps.

There was little resistance to the moves against their Jewish neighbours by the people of Germany. Many turned a blind eye while others were just pleased to see the country regaining its pride and its position as a power in Europe and the world. The 1936 Berlin Olympics had confirmed that status, even if the black American runner, Jesse Owens (1913–80) had upset Hitler's celebration of the Aryan race by winning four gold medals. Unemployment had been significantly reduced, even if large numbers of the once unemployed were now working in the munitions factories that were churning out arms in preparation for the war that many people knew must come. Hitler made no secret of his rearming of Germany and elements of military life began to seep into the everyday life of the German people. The *Hitler-Jugend* (Hitler Youth) and the *Deutches Jungvolk* (German Youth) prepared boys and young men to fight for their country, instilling in them the principles of Nazism. Nazi propaganda also prepared the German people for war.

At first, since Germany was still not strong enough to engage in military action, Hitler restricted himself, often very successfully, to the diplomatic front. However, a series of incidents began the path to war. In January 1935, the fifteen-year League of Nations mandate on the Saarland, the only part of Germany still under foreign control, came to an end. In a plebiscite to determine its future more than 90 per cent of the population expressed a desire to be returned to Germany. Then, in March, Hitler broke one of the terms of the Versailles Treaty when he introduced conscription. He followed that with a denunciation of the Treaties of Locarno and ordered his troops into the Rhineland which had been demilitarised in 1920 in order to create a buffer zone between Germany on one side and France, Belgium and Luxembourg on the other. On 12 March 1938, after several years of continuous pressure, he annexed Austria, in an action known as the *Anschluss*.

Britain, France and Italy had met in 1935 at Stresa in Italy to form a united front against German rearmament and to confirm the Locarno Treaties, but it was all to no avail. Britain, desperate to avoid war, embarked on a policy of appeasement towards Hitler and the Italians formed the Rome-Berlin Axis, following the signing of a treaty of friendship with the Germans in October 1936, welcoming Japan into the Axis and then Franco's Spain. France, meanwhile, was suffering internal problems posed by scandals and extremists.

For many, of course, Hitler was a useful bolster against communism and they were happy to let him get on with his expansionist plans. For others, the fear of war was so great that they were terrified to raise their voices. In 1938, Hitler's desire to annex the Sudetenland in Czechoslovakia and incorporate its largely ethnic German population into a Greater Germany brought Europe close to war. As German troops gathered on the border, preparing to invade, the British and French Prime Ministers, Neville Chamberlain and Georges Daladier, met with Hitler and Mussolini at Munich. Hitler claimed that this was his last territorial demand and an agreement was reached forcing the Czechs to cede the Sudetenland to Germany. Europe had been pulled back from the brink. On 15 March 1939, however, Hitler's true intentions became clear when he invaded the rest of Czechoslovakia. War was inevitable and Poland would be the catalyst.

The Second World War

Hitler had been agitating for some time about the German minority who lived in Poland but, on this occasion, the governments of Britain and France were unequivocal in their support for the Poles. However, it was unknown which way the Soviet Union would fall in the event of a German invasion of Poland. Following the death of Lenin in 1924 and a long period of infighting between bitter political rivals, the USSR had been ruled autocratically by Joseph Stalin (1878–1953) who had controlled his vast country using terror, a secret police force and show trials in which opponents of his regime confessed their guilt to the most unlikely of crimes. He established labour camps to house opponents or simply had them killed. Incredibly, in August 1939, Stalin signed a non-aggression pact with Hitler, but with good reason. Hitler was prepared to allow him a free hand in Poland and Eastern Europe. The Germans, in return, would benefit from not having to wage the impending war on two fronts.

On 3 September 1939, two days after German troops had marched into Poland, Britain and France declared war on Germany. Initially, however, they did nothing. Poland was rapidly beaten and the Russians occupied the eastern part of the country as agreed between Hitler and Stalin. Finland was next, the Soviets launching their attack on 30 November but, in a period known as the 'Phoney War', nothing much more happened until April 1940, when German troops occupied Denmark and Norway, breaching the neutrality of both countries. In the west, Belgium, Luxembourg and the Netherlands fell and, on 17 June 1940, after just six weeks of fighting, France capitulated. Britain stood alone. Meanwhile, Italy had invaded Albania in April and on 10 June declared war on Britain and France. Late October saw the Italians invade Greece where they met stiff opposition.

Just as Hitler began to believe in the summer of 1940 that Europe was his, he was forced to confront the determination of a British people galvanised by their charismatic leader, Winston Churchill (1874–1965). During the Battle of Britain, every major industrial British city was bombed but the RAF never lost its air superiority and the plan to weaken Britain from the air and then invade was abandoned.

Without warning, Hitler now launched an attack on the USSR on 22 June 1941 but, by the winter of 1941–42, his advance had been halted at Moscow and Leningrad. The war that Stalin named 'The Great Patriotic War' brought out the determination and courage of the Russian people as they staunchly resisted the German forces, especially at Stalingrad where, after months of street-fighting, the Germans capitulated. Around a million and a half people had died in the battle.

By now, all of Europe, apart from the neutral countries of Ireland, Switzerland, Spain, Portugal and Sweden, was at war. The conflict had also become a global conflagration with Japan's surprise attack on the US base at Pearl Harbor in December 1941. It was a war that involved everyone. Civilians had to endure massively destructive bombing raids on a daily basis and many took part in resistance movements, fighting clandestinely against occupying armies. General Charles de Gaulle led the Free French movement from London while, in Eastern Europe, partisans waged guerrilla warfare against their enemies.

In July 1943, the Allied invasion of Europe began in Sicily. It led to the capture of most of Italy. Mussolini was able to remain in power only precariously in the north, and with Hitler's support, before being shot by partisans in April 1945. D-Day, 6 June 1944, saw the Allies land in northern France and begin their advance on Berlin. The Red Army, meanwhile was ruthlessly advancing on Germany from the east. The final defeat of the Third Reich could be postponed but not avoided. On 30 April 1945, Hitler committed suicide in his bunker in Berlin and Germany surrendered eight days later. The war in Europe was over and, within months, the dropping of atomic bombs by the USA on Hiroshima and Nagasaki brought World War Two to an end.

The Casablanca, Teheran (both 1943) and Yalta (1945) Conferences had already given the Allied leaders the opportunity to make plans for after the war. Germany was divided between France, Britain, the USSR and the USA who would occupy and police their respective areas. Poland's frontier would be moved one hundred kilometres west and Russia would gain territory. The numbers who had died on one side or another in the years the war had lasted were even more staggering than those of the First World War. Some fifty to sixty million were dead or missing and many millions of those were civilians, killed by air raids or rampaging, occupying armies.

Europe was a continent in complete disarray. Entire peoples were displaced, having been either forcibly removed or obliged to flee before advancing armies. Europe was also bankrupt. Economies had been devastated by the funding of the war effort. Moreover, exhausted and broken, Europeans no longer found themselves at the centre of the universe. There was a new world order with two new superpowers – the United States of America and the USSR.

Towards a United Europe

Post-War Europe

As Europe crawled blinking from the ruins of World War Two, it was into the realisation that European domination of the world was at an end, a fact confirmed by the loss of its various colonial empires within two decades of the end of the war. The continent was bankrupt and entire cities lay in ruins. Large, formerly fertile areas, such as the Ukraine, had been devastated by fierce fighting. There were psychological scars, too. Nazi atrocities perpetrated against the Jews and others shocked an entire continent. The former superpowers of Europe were mere shadows of their former selves and the United States, its territory unblemished by warfare and its industry bolstered by the war effort, was now a leading player in the peace. So too was the Soviet Union, the might of its army undiminished by the fierce war it had just won.

The Soviets renewed their efforts to bring other countries in Eastern Europe into the communist sphere with the founding of Cominform, an official forum of the international communist movement. Stalin had convened this forum in 1947 in order to discuss the Marshall Plan, a programme devised by US Secretary of State, George Marshall, to rebuild Europe in the post-war period. Earlier that year, the British Prime Minister, Winston Churchill, had predicted the future when, during his *Sinews of*

Peace speech, delivered at Westminster College, Fulton, Mississippi, he said:

> From Stettin in the Baltic to Trieste in the Adriatic an 'iron curtain' has descended across the Continent. Behind that line lie all the capitals of the ancient states of Central and Eastern Europe. Warsaw, Berlin, Prague, Vienna, Budapest, Belgrade, Bucharest and Sofia; all these famous cities and the populations around them lie in what I must call the Soviet sphere, and all are subject, in one form or another, not only to Soviet influence but to a very high and in some cases increasing measure of control from Moscow.

A few months later, the refusal of the Russians and their satellites to accept the aid that came with the plan confirmed his vision and at once split the world in two, setting the scene for the next 45 years. A new war had begun, a war with many casualties, but no out-and-out fighting. American financier and US presidential adviser Bernard Baruch (1870–1965), came up with a name for this new war. He called it the 'Cold War'.

There was some opposition, of course, to communism. Czechoslovakia, for instance, was inclined to accept the US aid, but a communist coup in February 1948 put an end to that. There was also a bloody civil war in Greece between 1946 and 1949 that eventually defeated the communists who had played a major role in the liberation of the country.

The victorious powers had learned their lesson from the Treaty of Versailles at the end of the First World War and they tried desperately to solve the problems of what to do with Germany this time around without creating another major conflict within a few years. Berlin was a major flashpoint and the Soviets imposed a blockade on the city when the three Western occupying powers united their three zones and introduced a common currency in June 1948 – the Deutschmark. The Allies began the Berlin airlift, supplying their zones with essentials by air. The blockade was only lifted after a year. Then, in May 1949, the Soviets became even more inflamed when the Washington Agreement established the Federal Republic of Germany (West Germany) with its capital in Bonn. On 7 October, the Russians announced the founding of the German Democratic Republic (East Germany) in their zone.

Fear of war continued. NATO, the North Atlantic Treaty Organisation, had been created in 1949 to provide a system of collective defence and there was even a suggestion of allowing West Germany to rearm and become a member of a putative European army, proposed by the French, consisting of troops from France, Luxembourg, Belgium, Italy and the Netherlands. The European Defence Community (EDC), one of the first real modern efforts at European unity, failed to come into being, however, when the French National Assembly refused to ratify it. The Western European Union took its place in 1954 and this time Britain was involved. West Germany became a member and in 1955 became a full member of NATO. Not to be outdone, the USSR responded a few months later with its own military union – the Warsaw Pact.

Decolonisation

The term 'Third World' was coined by the French demographer Alfred Sauvy in 1952. He wrote in an article in the French magazine, *L'Observateur* of the colonised countries:

> ... at the end this ignored, exploited, scorned Third World, like the Third Estate, wants to become something too.

Indeed it did, and it expressed its desire at a conference in Bandung in Indonesia in 1955 when 29 Asian and African nations met to declare their demand for decolonisation.

The Russians were supportive of their demand but only to the extent that independence for the colonies would serve to damage the colonial powers. Meanwhile, the United States refrained from upsetting its western allies, although, in principle, it favoured decolonisation. Both superpowers displayed their support when they agreed to lift their ban on new members being allowed to join the United Nations, the organisation that had been set up in 1945 to replace the largely ineffectual League of Nations.

Decolonisation began at a pace and had varying effects on the colonial powers. Britain granted India independence in 1947, the country being split into two nations, India and Pakistan. The British created the Commonwealth in 1949, a largely powerless organisation containing Britain and many of its former colonies. In 1960, a dozen African colonies won independence from Britain and throughout the 1960s the process continued. By 1975, when the Portuguese left Angola after a lengthy war of independence, the European hold on countries and territories across the world that had begun five centuries earlier was almost over.

The only country initially to stand aloof from the process of decolonisation was France which wanted to retain its hold on its colonies as a sign that it was still a major power. It soon received two major blows to its pride. The first came in Indo-China where the communist leader Ho Chi Minh fought for independence for Vietnam from 1945 until 1954 when the French were beaten at Dien Bien Phu. The second occurred over France's intractable Algerian problem. Charles de Gaulle, elected French president in 1958, divested himself of the problem after a great deal of violence when he signed the Evian Agreements in 1962.

Europe no longer controlled the world. Indeed, to some extent, it could be said the world now controlled Europe. When Egyptian President Gamal Abdel Nasser nationalised the Suez Canal in July 1956, it was brought home to the former mighty powers of Europe just how far they had fallen in the world pecking order. France and Britain linked with Israel to regain control of the canal and at first enjoyed some success against Egyptian troops. When the USSR became involved, threatening to use nuclear weapons against Britain and France and the United States refused to help, the British and French had little option but to withdraw with their tails between their legs.

Eastern Europe

After the war, the Soviet Union rapidly extended its influence over the nations of Eastern Europe. East Germany, Poland, Czechoslovakia, Romania, Bulgaria, Hungary and Albania all fell into the Soviet sphere of influence, allying themselves with the USSR and with each other. Communist governments were established in all of them, and they were known as 'People's Democracies'. Other political parties were banned and Cominform formed a necessary link.

The only leader to stand up to the Soviets was Josip Broz Tito (1892–1980), leader of the Socialist Federal Republic of Yugoslavia and an armed confrontation was narrowly avoided as Tito pursued his own policies, becoming a founder member of the non-aligned movement. Other leaders who displayed national-ist tendencies were quickly dealt with so that their countries could not follow the same 'Titoist' path as Yugoslavia. Polish leader Wladyslaw Gomulka (1905–82) was sacked in 1948, Hungarian leader Laszlo Rajk (1909–49) was hanged in 1949 and, in 1952, Czech leader Rudolf Slansky (1901–52) was also hanged, after a show trial.

The Soviet satellite states entered into economic cooperation with the USSR and were forced to introduce reforms imitating the Soviet system – nationalisation, collectivisation and agrarian reform. Press freedom was abolished and a Communist elite was cultivated in each country. Art and culture were strictly controlled. Painting, for instance, had to adhere to the tenets of 'Socialist Realism'. The Church was repressed and senior members of the clergy were arrested and incarcerated.

When Stalin died in 1953, people became less afraid of voicing criticism of the regime, although this often still resulted in expulsion from the party and isolation. New Secretary General of the Communist Party, Nikita Khrushchev initiated a programme of de-Stalinisation and the way was open for individual states within the Soviet sphere to devise their own types of Socialism. There was still discontent, however, and 1956 saw revolt against the Soviet regime in Poland and in Hungary. In Poland, former leader Gomulka, purged by Stalin in 1948, returned to power but in Hungary, leader Imre Nagy (1896–1958) planned to restore private property and reinstate the Catholic Church. On 4 September, Soviet troops occupied Budapest and ruthlessly crushed all resistance, replacing Nagy with János Kádár (1912–89).

Russia had delivered a powerful message to its satellites about how far they would be allowed to go. When they tried to stem the flood of refugees from East Berlin to West Berlin by building a wall separating the two halves of the city in August 1961, it gave solid form to Churchill's metaphorical 'iron curtain'.

A Common Market

After the end of the war, European unity was seen as one way of avoiding the reappearance of the type of nationalism that had so recently devastated the continent. The first sign of such cooperation came with the founding in April 1948 of the Organisation for European Economic Cooperation (OEEC), the body that would distribute the massive amount of aid provided by the American Marshall Plan. Between 1948 and 1952, European countries received some $13,000 million, Britain receiving more than $3,000 million, France $2,700 million, Italy $1,474 million and Germany $1,389 million. In 1960, it would become the Organisation for Economic Cooperation and Development (OECD), consisting of 30 member states dedicated to the principles of representative democracy and free-market economy.

Other organisations such as the European Coal and Steel Community, whose founding members were Belgium, France, Italy, Luxembourg, the Netherlands and West Germany – was claimed in the *Schuman Declaration* of 9 May 1950, made by French Foreign Minister, Robert Schuman, to be 'a first step in a federation of Europe' and proved the value of cooperation between European states. Britain stayed out in order to protect its sovereignty and to prevent friction with members of the British Commonwealth.

The International Committee of the Movements for European Unity held a Congress of Europe in 1948, chaired by none other than Winston Churchill, which called for a political and economic union in Europe, a European Assembly and a European Court of Human Rights. The Council of Europe was established as a result to deal with legal standards, human rights, democratic development, the rule of law and cultural co-operation. In 1950, it published the European Convention for the Protection of Human Rights.

Further European cooperation emerged in the age-old problem of the Saarland which, although under French control since the war, expressed its desire once again in a referendum to be part of Germany. This duly happened in 1956 but this time without trouble. Europe, it seemed, had grown up and was beginning to view things in a continent-wide context, rather than in a purely national one.

The Birth of the European Union

Many had dreamed of uniting Europe and, indeed, large parts of it had enjoyed some form of union during the continent's long history – the Roman Empire, the Frankish Empire, the Holy Roman Empire, the Napoleonic Empire and Hitler's Nazi Germany had all brought together large areas of the European continent, but usually by force of arms and in unions that were neither willing nor mutually beneficial. The idea of such a geopolitical entity had been considered before, of course. In the seventeenth century, William Penn (1644–1718), founder of the Province of Pennsylvania, the English North American colony, advocated a 'United States of Europe'. The eighteenth-century French Enlightenment writer and radical, Abbé Charles de Saint Pierre (1658–1743), wrote about an international court and league of states. In the nineteenth century, Italian politician and philosopher, Giuseppe Mazzini (1805–72), a leading player in the unification of Italy, used his experience in that struggle to advocate a unified Europe. In 1941, Hungarian Prime Minister, Pál Teleki, devised a plan for a European federation, based on geographical and economic realities, shortly before he committed suicide in the face of Nazi aggression against his country. Winston Churchill, too, had called for a United States of Europe in 1946 and America favoured European Union and worked to try to make it happen, creating organisations such as the American Committee on United Europe and the European Youth Campaign.

In 1957, following the success of the European Coal and Steel Community, the Treaties of Rome were signed by France, West Germany, Luxembourg, Belgium and the Netherlands, establishing the European Economic Community (EEC) and the European Atomic Energy Community (Euratom). The basis for the EEC was a customs union, wherein members charged no customs tariffs to each other and shared a common customs tariff with regard to outside states. Having initially refused to join the EEC, Britain made an attempt to establish a free trade community whose members would include all the countries who were part of the Organisation for European Economic Development. When the plan was rejected, principally by France, Britain and six other countries who had not been admitted to the EEC – Denmark, Norway, Portugal, Sweden, Austria and Switzerland – formed their own trade organisation, the European Free Trade Association (EFTA).

The EEC, known as the Common Market, came into operation on 1 January 1958 and had soon become an important and successful organisation. Amongst its plans for the future was a common agricultural policy as well as economic and monetary union. Britain applied for membership of the EEC twice – in 1963 and 1967 – but was rebuffed on each occasion by French President, Charles de Gaulle, who feared that British membership would introduce damaging American influence into the organisation.

The West Prospers and the East Stagnates

During the 1960s, good times seemed to have come to Western Europe. Year-on-year economic growth and increased trade with the rest of the world brought unheard-of prosperity to its countries and peoples. Numerous medical advances and technological innovation brought longer life and greater happiness. Wages increased, purchasing power doubling in ten years, and a great deal of money was being spent on labour-saving items such as washing machines and what were seen then as luxury items – refrigerators, televisions, telephones and hi-fi systems. For the first time, home-ownership spread and there was a building boom. People were able to take holidays, often abroad, and indulge in other leisure activities. Everyone became middle class, or behaved as if they were, and real poverty was now to be found in specific social groupings – immigrants, the unskilled, the uneducated and the elderly.

In 1942, the British economist and social reformer, William Beveridge (1879–1963), produced a report for the British government that identified the five 'Giant Evils' in society as 'squalor, ignorance, want, idleness and disease'. The government took steps after the war to deal with these issues, including the introduction of the Welfare State in an attempt to at least make medical treatment available to all, 'from the cradle to the grave' and 'free at the point of use'. It was a policy that would have great influence on other European states, social security in particular being generally adopted.

The state also intervened in other ways in many Western European countries, nationalisation becoming an important element of economic policy. State ownership of energy, transport and banks enabled them to exercise greater national economic control. State involvement in technology would lead to international ventures such as the building of a supersonic airliner, the Concorde, in a joint venture involving Britain and France and the European Space Agency's satellite launcher, *Ariane*, which put more than 50 satellites into space.

Meanwhile in the Soviet Union, the opposite was happening. Russia had put the first man into space on 12 April 1961 when Soviet cosmonaut, Yuri Gagarin made one orbit of the earth, but the liberalisers had lost out when Premier, Nikita Khrushchev, was dismissed and replaced by the reactionary Leonid Brezhnev whose 'Brezhnev Doctrine' sought to bring the USSR and its satellites into line. Several of these satellites were, however, suffering from social and economic problems and one, in particular, expressed its disillusionment in an uprising. As Czech intellectuals agitated for radical reform, Alexander Dubček, purged in the 1950s, returned to power. His 'Socialism with a human face' was anathema to the USSR and, echoing Hungary in 1956, Warsaw Pact tanks rolled in to crush the 'Prague Spring' in 1968. Rioting in Poland also had to be crushed in 1970, emphasising still further how tenuous the Soviet grip on Eastern Europe was becoming.

A New Attitude

Rationing and food shortages had persisted in Europe for many years after the war and a generation grew up with hardship and poverty as everyday companions. The affluent consumer society that began to develop in the colourful 1960s following the dour, monotone 1950s brought huge changes to society and the family. The new music, launched in the mid-1950s by American rocker, Elvis Presley, and developed by the English beat group The Beatles in the 1960s, created a huge international youth movement. Suddenly teenagers seemed like alien beings to their parents, their colourful, sexy clothing contrasting greatly with the utilitarian garb of their own youth. As the 1960s progressed, the youth of Europe found its voice in other ways than through music. It became politicised and protested against numerous things but principally American involvement in the Vietnam War. Dissatisfaction in France at the de Gaulle government erupted in violent protests by students and workers in May 1968 that would culminate in the resignation of de Gaulle the following year.

One of the most significant changes in society was the increasing role that women played. Throughout the twentieth century the position of women in society had gradually evolved – war work had brought them out from behind the cooker in both world wars and courageous campaigns had finally brought them the vote. Now they demanded equal rights as citizens, both in the workplace and in their private lives. Feminist movements were founded which campaigned for the right to abortion and divorce. The contraceptive pill created a sexual revolution and gave women control of their sexual lives for the first time.

The Catholic Church reeled in the face of the moral revolution that was sweeping Europe and the rest of the developed world. The Second Vatican Council met from 1962 to 1965, dealing with many issues including a familiar one – the celibacy of priests. It determined that the vernacular could be introduced into the liturgy, instead of Latin, and that national or local customs could also be incorporated. However, it failed to stem the decline in church attendance and religious observation in an increasingly secular world.

The 1970s: Economic Chaos and Social Unrest

All good things must come to an end and they did in the 1970s when Europe's consistent growth was brought to an abrupt conclusion by several factors. The first was the 1971 collapse of the international financial system devised by the Bretton Woods Conference in 1944, destabilising world trade and financial dealings. The second was the increase in the price of oil in 1973 after an Arab-Israeli war and the nationalisation of Western companies' oil installations in OPEC countries. Further oil price rises occurred in 1979. Industry suffered and European industry in particular, long reliant on cheap energy sources, was exposed as outdated and uncompetitive. The result was inflation and recession in many sectors of industry such as car production. There was a serious increase in unemployment and conditions were ripe for the rise once more of extreme far-right political parties as immigration was blamed in many cases for the lack of jobs.

In mainstream politics there was also change. In Britain, the governing Labour Party was replaced by the Conservatives in 1979, led by Britain's first woman Prime Minister, Margaret Thatcher (b. 1925). The socialists also lost in Germany when Helmut Kohl's (b. 1930) Christian Democrats defeated the Social Democrats. In France, however, the socialist, François Mitterrand (1916–96) bucked the trend by becoming President in 1981.

Meanwhile, a number of dictatorships passed quietly into history. In Greece the Colonels, who had ruled since 1967, relinquished power; in Portugal, Antonio Salazar died in 1970 and the dictatorial regime that had replaced him was ended by the Carnation Revolution led by a left-leaning military junta in 1974, which brought democracy within two years. In Spain, the dictatorship of General Franco finally came to an end with his death in 1975 and the restoration of the monarchy.

Political radicalism erupted around this time in several parts of Europe, often in response to the harsh economic climate and as a blow against the capitalist system. The Red Army Faction, also known as the Baader-Meinhof Group, in Germany and the Red Brigades in Italy perpetrated outrages against society — taking hostages, kidnapping and murdering. In Britain and Spain, the IRA and ETA, respectively, waged war on government. In Northern Ireland, the Troubles that had erupted in the late 1960s continued, spreading to the rest of the United Kingdom with a bombing campaign that killed or maimed many people while ETA mounted a campaign in Spain.

The European Union: Expansion

The EEC continued with its development, despite a six-month period when President de Gaulle refused to attend meetings (the so-called 'policy of the empty chair') in protest at efforts at integration. In 1967, the ECSC, EEC and Euratom were merged into one body and the customs union was achieved earlier than anticipated. On 1 January 1973, it finally accepted new members – Britain, Denmark and Ireland. The oil crisis provoked an immediate challenge for the newly enlarged organisation and the British asked to renegotiate its terms of membership in 1974, following the election of a Labour government. A 1975 referendum confirmed Britain's membership with two-thirds of voters opting to remain part of the Community.

The European Monetary System (EMS) was established in 1979 but Britain opted out and, a few years later, Margaret Thatcher obtained compensation for a budget contribution she considered too high. The European Council, a meeting of heads of state and governments, was established in 1974 and, in 1976, it was decided that the European Parliament should be elected by universal suffrage. In 1985, the Schengen Agreement created open borders with no passport controls between some member states. In 1986, the Single European Act was signed, establishing the Single European Market. Six years later, the European Union was created by the Maastricht Treaty.

Coming in From the Cold: The Fall of the Berlin Wall

Willy Brandt (1913–92), former Mayor of West Berlin, was elected Chancellor of West Germany in 1969. As Chancellor, he developed *Ostpolitik*, a policy with the objective of improving relations with his neighbours, East Germany and Poland, as well as with the Soviet Union. It became part of a series of conciliatory acts. In 1971, the USA, USSR, France and Britain agreed to make contact between East and West Berlin easier. Brandt also devised a treaty by which a number of Western states recognised East Germany, with the result that both East and West Germany became members of the United Nations in 1973. Then, Cold War tensions were further reduced in 1975 by the Helsinki Conference on Security and Cooperation in Europe which arrived at an important consensus on a number of issues, such as the recognition of European borders as decided at the end of the Second World War.

Nonetheless, agitation grew in the east, perhaps now helped by Helsinki's bold statements about human rights. Czechoslovakia, slapped down in the 1970s, continued to smoulder with suppressed dissent and the Charter 77 group continued to protest. It was in Poland, however, that the greatest unrest occurred, perhaps encouraged by the tide of national feeling engendered by the election of Carol Wojtyla (1920–2005) as Pope John Paul II in 1978, the first non-Italian Pope since Adrian VI in 1522. In 1980, the shipyard workers in Gdansk, members of the free trade union, *Solidarność* (Solidarity), rebelled under the leadership of Lech Wałęsa (b.1943), with the support of the Catholic Church in Poland. Within a year, the union had ten million members. Polish authorities, led by General Wojciech Jaruzelski (b.1923), moved to ban it and arrested its leaders.

Mikhail Gorbachev (b.1931) was elected Secretary General of the Soviet Communist Party in 1985 following the deaths in rapid succession of Brezhnev and his two successors, Yuri Andropov (1914–84) and Konstantin Chernenko (1911–85). Gorbachev was a reformer and championed the concepts of *glasnost* (openness) and *perestroika* (restructuring) with which he hoped to bring socialism back to life in the east. In 1989, he announced that the Soviet Union would no longer stand in the way of any of its satellite states that wished to change their way of government and the nations of the east did not stand on ceremony, most dismantling the Communist apparatus and holding elections that same year.

In Poland, Solidarity won the first free elections held in the country since the 1930s and, in 1990, Lech Wałęsa became president; Hungary became a republic and held free elections; in the 'Velvet Revolution', Czechoslovakia became a democracy under the presidency of the playwright, Vaclav Havel and Slovakia and the Czech Republic, forcibly brought together at the end of the First World War, soon became separate states; in Romania, the ruthless dictator Nicolae Ceauçescu and his wife were arrested and executed and democracy was introduced; in Bulgaria and Albania, the communists succeeded in retaining power as members of coalition governments.

Events were most dramatic in East Germany where the Berlin Wall was a concrete symbol of the division of Europe and of the German people. As the reform movement spread throughout Eastern Europe, demonstrations and civil unrest broke out in East Germany. Leader Erich Honecker (1912–94) resigned and his replacements made the decision to throw open the borders. On 9 November 1989, people began to take sledgehammers to the Berlin Wall and Germany was united once again.

The Balkans Erupt

The twentieth century ended as it had begun, with bloodshed in the Balkans. At the end of the First World War, the Treaty of Versailles had cobbled together a state to house the Southern Slavs, consisting of the Serbs, the Croats and the Slovenes. In 1929, it had become the Kingdom of Yugoslavia and then, after the Second World War, the Socialist Federal Republic of Yugoslavia, made up of a number of Socialist Republics – Bosnia-Herzegovina, Croatia, Macedonia, Montenegro, Serbia and Slovenia.

The spirit of independence in the air towards the end of the 1980s made the Croats and Slovenes want independence, too. The Serbs tried to stop them and went to war with their old enemies, the Croats, besieging Zagreb and shelling the ancient port and tourist attraction of Dubrovnik. Then, when Bosnia-Herzegovina also declared independence in 1992, the Serbs, in one of the most shameful and horrific episodes since the Second World War, tried to ethnically cleanse the area of Croats and Muslims. Many thousands of men were rounded up, shot and buried in mass graves, most notably at Srebreniça where troops of General Ratko Mladić (b. 1942) massacred 8,000 Bosnian Muslims. Eventually, following United Nations intervention, Serbia was forced to accept the independence of Bosnia-Herzegovina. The other republics have since gained their independence, the most recent being Kosovo, which declared independence in February 2008, although Serbia and a number of other nations have yet to recognise the new nation.

Europe in the Twenty-first Century

As the twenty-first century dawned, the European Union was well-established, although there was still considerable griping about it, most noticeably from those on the right in Britain. It was made up of 27 member states – Austria, Belgium, Bulgaria, Cyprus, the Czech Republic, Denmark, Estonia, Finland, France, Germany, Greece, Hungary, the Republic of Ireland, Italy, Latvia, Lithuania, Luxembourg, Malta, the Netherlands, Poland, Portugal, Romania, Slovakia, Slovenia, Spain, Sweden and the United Kingdom. It had its own parliament and the European Commission, its executive branch, with 27 commissioners responsible for legislation, implementation and the day-to-day business of the Union, effectively acted as an international government. In 2002, another milestone was reached when 12 member states replaced their currencies with the euro, another three following later.

There have been setbacks, however. The European Constitution was rejected in referenda in 2005 by Dutch and French voters and, requiring ratification by all member states before it is adopted, has been abandoned, to be replaced by a Reform Treaty. The Treaty of Lisbon, designed to streamline the workings of the European Union, was also rejected when the Irish voted against it in a referendum in June 2008. But, the European Union has done the job it was set up for, fostering partnership amongst nations and, let us not forget, helping to prevent Europe from descending into the kind of continent-wide conflagration that killed so many during the twentieth century.

History, as the twentieth century so adequately proved, is cyclical, and there is some irony in the fact that in this new century we once again look beyond our borders and our own western ideology at a similar threat to the one faced by the Holy Roman Emperors of medieval times. Al-Qaeda and global terrorists, and not the Saracens, the Magyars, the Vikings or the Mongols are the new threat and although there is little possibility of them invading our territories, the damage they can do is incalculable as proved by the World Trade Center atrocity in New York in 2001 and Europe's very own experience of terrorist horror in Madrid and London in 2004 and 2007, respectively. In the east, too, the tanks have been rolling again, as Russia crushes rebellion in Chechnya and South Ossetia.

Plus ça change, you might say, and you would be right.

Further Reading

Robert Bartlett, *The Making of Europe*, London: Allen Lane, 1993

TCW Blanning, *The Oxford Illustrated History of Modern Europe*, Oxford: Oxford University Press, 1996

John Hale, *Renaissance Europe 1480–1520*, London: Fontana, 1971

Norman Hampson, *The Enlightenment*, London: Penguin, 1968

EJ Hobsbawm, *The Age of Revolution: Europe 1789–1848*, London: Weidenfeld & Nicolson, 1962

EJ Hobsbawm, *The Age of Capital: Europe 1848–1875* London: Weidenfeld & Nicolson, 1975

EJ Hobsbawm, *The Age of Empire: Europe 1875–1914* London: Weidenfeld & Nicolson, 1978

George Holmes, *The Oxford Illustrated History of Medieval Europe*, Oxford: Oxford University Press, 1988

James Joll, *Europe Since 1870*, London: Weidenfeld & Nicolson, 1973

Tony Judt, *Postwar: A History of Europe Since 1945*, London: William Heinemann, 2006

Mark Mazower, *Dark Continent: Europe's Twentieth Century*, London: Allen Lane, 1998

JM Roberts, *Europe 1880–1945*, London: Longmans, 1967

JM Roberts, *The Penguin History of Europe*, London: Penguin, 1997

David Thomson, *Europe Since Napoleon*, London: Longmans, 1957

Index

INDEX

INDEX

INDEX